JIMMY NEWELL

ISBN: 1490414010
ISBN 13: 9781490414010

Eileen,
always it's you.

PREFACE

It has often been said that a life worth living is a life worth recording. My life is worth recording because I have been blessed with the grace of extraordinary friends and a beloved family. We are not alone on life's journey. *A Bronx Boy's Tale* is an affirmation of this truth, and it is also the record of my life as seen through my eyes and absorbed through my heart. While I have poetically (I hope) distorted the precise truth, the fundamental truth remains intact.

Most of the events occurred as written. Some have been romanticized to allow the story to flow, but even in the instances where the truth has been stretched, the spirit of those events remains unaltered.

I wanted to tell my story of growing up in the Bronx. I wanted to preserve a memory that has been shared by thousands of others who lived in God's own land at a very special time. But there are other reasons for writing about growing up in the Bronx in the 1960s and 70s.

During one of the games of the 1977 World Series (a World Series that the Yankees won), the TV camera panned off the field of play and onto the surreal sight of the Bronx on fire. Having recently left the Bronx for the distant, foreign, land of Flushing, the image saddened and embarrassed me at the same time. A Bronx boy is forever a Bronx boy. That scene was broadcast across the country and probably around the world, and I resented the fact that many people would forever think of that fire as the true nature of the Bronx.

Additional motivation to write my life story was provided by the scandals that have nearly destroyed the Catholic Church. Blessed Sacrament, the parish where I was raised, provided the backdrop of my life. I met my best friends while attending Blessed Sacrament. Blessed Sacrament formed a common history for my wife and me despite the fact that I was four years older. We all grew up with common experiences, and most of us with a lot of love.

Lay teachers and nuns taught us, and we were always in the company of priests who were the social and athletic directors of our neighborhood. Not one person I knew has ever claimed to have been sexually abused. One or two may have been smacked and tackled, and we all had the fear of God firmly implanted in our conscious and subconscious selves, but back then, who didn't have that experience?

I want to let the world know that the priests and nuns we had in Blessed Sacrament were excellent role models, and gave us much that many still hold as important and sacred.

All of my friends have remained close to each other nearly fifty years after we left Blessed Sacrament. It is a shame and a real loss to the community that Blessed Sacrament School will be shutting its doors.

A Bronx Boy's Tale is about life as it once was. It's about a life that lives on for those of us who remember it, and I hope this memoir captures its essence.

A Bronx Boy's Tale is my testament that I wanted to preserve for my children. While they may be disappointed in the dollar amount of my legacy, I am hoping that the stories will be rewarding enough to make up for their financial shortfall. Stories are what I have to give, as those of you who know me can attest.

Jimmy Newell

http://www.jim-newellpost.com/

TABLE OF CONTENTS

CHAPTER 1

ROMANTIC MUSKETEERS

I awoke that November morning humming a tune. It was Friday, and I was thirteen. The fact that I had to go to school didn't bother me as much as it had my previous seven years at Blessed Sacrament. School no longer meant endless hours of mind-numbing boredom interspersed with periods of angst and good, old-fashioned terror. Oh, I still had some angst, and there was always a little bit of terror, but now school also provided my ultimate elation in life, and in truth, the only opportunity to see Kathy. And someday soon, I knew that I would even get to talk to her.

No one in my family had the faintest inkling of my new attitude toward school, or of my someday-soon-to-be love, as I did my utmost to keep such things to myself. Notwithstanding my aforementioned pedagogical renaissance, my mother continued facing the daily challenge of getting me up and off to school after forcing me to scarf down some oatmeal. She didn't know that my inability to eat breakfast was no longer related to pre-school nausea as it used to be; it was now lovesickness.

In keeping with tradition, I remained my surly self in the first few moments after waking up. This was due mostly to sleep deprivation brought on by listening to my transistor radio into the wee hours of the morning. So, as far as my family was concerned, all things were as they should be, except for the humming.

My mother noticed it first, and after repeated (though unheeded) pleas to "Stop that blasted humming," she finally took me by the shoulders. Then she calmly said in her rich Irish brogue, which was only discernable to my friends for some reason, "Luv, if you don't stop that, I'm going to slap your backside all the way down to DALLAS."

As you might imagine, she immediately got my attention, and I hummed that tune no more. For the life of me, I couldn't figure out why I was humming a song like that in the first place. Maybe I heard it on the radio or on *Ed Sullivan*, but surely Cousin Brucie or Murray the K hadn't played it last night. All the New York radio stations that I listened to were playing the Four Seasons, Beach Boys, and a new group from England, of all places, whose song was, in fact, the reason for my late night radio listening.

Just before midnight, I heard "I Want to Hold Your Hand" on WABC, and immediately began what might one day be called surfing the dial. After hearing that song the first time, I went immediately to WMCA, WINS, and back to WABC hoping to hear it one more time. That's why waking up humming "Big D" was as much a mystery to me as it was annoying to my mother. But on this day, Friday, November 22, 1963, with the prospect of seeing Kathy, I deftly knotted my blue, Catholic school-issued tie, put on my suit jacket and coat, and made my way to Blessed Sacrament without another thought about Dallas.

As I left my apartment on 1261 Leland Avenue, the Pelham Bay downtown express rumbled on the EL on Westchester Avenue. I turned in the opposite direction and walked toward Gleason Avenue. As I proceeded to school, I surveyed all that was before me and thought I was in Paradise. What could be better than a cool, crisp autumn day in the Bronx? In addition to being perfect football weather, it was Friday; next week was Thanksgiving, and then the Christmas season would begin. The agony of early fall and the Yankees getting swept by the Dodgers in the World Series was but a distant memory, and now it had been replaced by a new agony, though a bit more pleasant. Love was in the air on Leland Avenue.

My reveries were interrupted by the problem at hand. Should I hustle my way to school or should I drag my feet? I wasn't worried about being late for school, as I had left early enough for the short walk to Blessed Sacrament School (BSS). My dilemma was timing my walk so that I might run into Kathy on her way to school.

Kathy's house was just down the block from mine, but sometimes she would get a ride to school. So, even on the days when I timed my walk perfectly, I sometimes felt a heartbreak that only a black 1958 Mercury backing out of a driveway could cause. As I approached her house, I instinctively looked up the long driveway that went along the side of her house to the backyard. However, instead of the taillights of the Mercury making its way down the driveway, I saw a behemoth of a dog lumbering toward me closely followed by a screaming and frantic Kathy.

Even in my startled state of impending doom, I could not help but note how beautiful she was. Mine was a recent appreciation, and I could not determine, for the life of me, how all of a sudden she had become so gorgeous. As kids, we played together even before we entered first grade, but I never thought of her as beautiful. In fact, for the first seven years of grammar school, I'm not sure I was even aware that we still lived on the same block. Then we turned thirteen and wham—she was suddenly beautiful!

Now, I couldn't stop thinking that she was the most beautiful girl I'd ever seen, and I thought about her all the time—well, almost all the time. Right now, I was thinking about the charging mongrel that was sizing me up for breakfast. However, what happened next altered my sentiment regarding this flea-bitten beast.

Kathy was commanding the dog to stop, but he must have thought she meant run as fast as you can, you dear, little doggy. When she realized her efforts were fruitless, Kathy stopped yelling at the dog and yelled at me. "Jimmy, get him!" There's nothing like a command from a forceful woman to make you feel loved and needed. Could this day get any better?

With a thud, I rose, or it might be more accurate to say collapsed to the occasion as I allowed my damsel's runaway steed to play Johnny on the Pony with me on the short end. Despite my unorthodox method of corralling her beast, Kathy rewarded me with the most beautiful of phrases ever uttered on Leland Avenue. "Thanks a lot, Jimmy," she said, and then she made her way back up the driveway dragging the dog by the collar.

I just lay there in the driveway repeating those words of love in my head. So caught up in the passion, I barely heard the motor of the Mercury as it rolled toward me. Eventually, the rumbling of the old car interrupted my musings just in time for me to roll over to the side and avoid the rear wheels.

I scrambled to my feet and out of harm's way realizing I would not fare as well in a collision with this marvel of American engineering as I had with the old mutt. As I was dusting myself off and collecting my book bag, I caught a fleeting glimpse of Kathy sitting in the front seat next to her mother. I stood there in awe for a few seconds before making my way to school. I had achieved my goal of seeing Kathy. Now more than ever, I was determined that the next time our paths crossed, I was actually going to speak to her.

After arriving at school, I joined the usual cohort of hooligans, namely Mike, PJ, and Trent. As friends go, they are the best: honest enough to let you know when you have something hanging off your nose, compassionate enough to stop laughing after only five or ten minutes. We were all in the eighth grade, but we had other things to talk about that were more important than school. Our pre-school discussion centered on football—what else? Well, I guess it could have been girls, but football was easier to understand so early in the morning.

Today's game, as always, would be at 3:30 p.m. on Thieriot Avenue in front of Laura's house. Laura was also an eighth-grader and was the subject of Mike's affection and attention. He had the hots for her. She was also best friends with Kathy, so with that in my mind, the four of us made a beautiful couple.

Then suddenly, Sister Irene Mary appeared out of nowhere. She approached our little sewing circle, and from somewhere deep within the innermost recesses of the robes of her black nun's habit, she withdrew a hand grasping a bell. The vigor with which she rang that bell brought to mind a blacksmith hammering out a piece of molten iron.

Standing so close to her meant that our ears would ring throughout religion class and halfway into arithmetic. Needless to say, Sister Irene achieved her goal. It's always a marvel to see six hundred screaming kids suddenly brought to an instantaneous silence. Even the future hoods and criminals of BSS were careful not to breach the silence of the first bell.

The second bell, somewhat softer and of a lower pitch, signaled that the four upper grades housed in the new school should proceed to their classrooms. I was in 8A 3, Sister Margaret's class, which was on the top floor at the opposite end of the hall from 8A 1 and 8A 2. Kathy and Laura were in 8A 1 along with PJ and Trent, and Mike was in 8A 2. I sat in the first row facing the door alongside one of the wall-length blackboards. Thus, I was strategically situated to catch a glimpse of Kathy if she happened to stand in the right spot when our two classroom doors and one of the swinging doors in the middle of the corridor were all opened at the same time. The fact that the odds of this happening were akin to the linear alignment of the nine known planets did not dampen my enthusiasm for looking up every time I heard the door open.

Sister Margaret walked into the classroom, and we took our seats. She was a great teacher and did not fit the image that we had of nuns as angry tormentors of little children. She was always smiling and would even chuckle from time to time. Sister Margaret gave us much more freedom than even some of our lay teachers gave us when we were in the lower grades, and she would often stray from the curriculum when she had a good story to tell. She especially liked to tell us of her experiences as a nun in Nassau in the Bahamas. This particular morning was rather uneventful. We whizzed through religion and arithmetic, and soon it was time for art with Miss O'Neil.

The great thing about Miss O'Neil, especially if you were a clumsy artist like me, was that she had a short memory. Very often, she would walk around the class and stop by my desk to help me draw a color wheel or do some other project. She would just about do the whole thing before moving on. Then when she came back to review all our work, she would tell the class what a lovely job I had done. She also gave us small copies of famous paintings so that we never had to go to a museum. You had to love that!

After we cleared our desks of our art materials, it was time for history. We were studying the Industrial Revolution, specifically discussing how the railroad helped to create national markets for the coal and steel industries. We learned all about the famous men of the time including Andrew Carnegie and Cornelius Vanderbilt. Sister Margaret described these and others as robber barons. Then, before we knew it, Sister Irene Mary was reciting the Angelus and the blessing before meals over the PA system, and we were off to lunch.

Some of us ate lunch in the school cafeteria and others went home. Not having as good a sense of humor when it came to food, I went home for lunch. I tried the cafeteria back in the fifth grade for one week, which was more than enough. What the cafeteria food lacked in taste, it more than made up for in mystery. While my unfortunate friends tried to determine if they were eating tuna fish or not, I was faced with the more enviable decision of whether to have peanut butter and jelly or cream cheese and jelly. Since it was Friday, bologna was off the menu despite all my well-reasoned efforts to convince my mother that cow's hooves, lips, and other unmentionable body parts did not come under the papal edict for meatless Fridays.

We had about forty minutes for lunch, and then it was back to class for our weekly spelling test. The afternoon dragged until, thankfully, Sister Margaret handed out the week's *Young Catholic Messenger*. This was a magazine with short articles about current events and other topics. We were allowed to read this quietly to ourselves until one thirty, when we would have a group discussion on some of the articles we read.

Like everyone else in the class, I turned to the back page first, which had a joke section. I didn't hear anyone laugh, so I imagined that everyone found this week's entries as stupid as I did. I then turned to a story about the future. It described how people in the twenty-first century would have to wear space suits because the earth's atmosphere would be so polluted. Next came sports.

The annual Army-Navy game was coming up, and though I was a Notre Dame fan, I read an article about President Kennedy attending the game. Since he was the commander-in-chief, he would sit on Army's side for the first half and then Navy's for the second half. They wouldn't even let him watch a game in peace.

Sister Margaret then got our attention and we discussed some of the things we had just read. Even though Kathy wasn't in my class, I did my best to be clever whenever the opportunity presented itself. I had learned back in sixth grade that the surest way to a woman's heart is by dropping a funny line at just the right moment. This was an absolute necessity for those of us not blessed with being overly cute. So, as we began our discussion, I was armed and ready with a few well-chosen witticisms hoping they would somehow be relayed to Kathy later that day. But no sooner had we begun than Sister Irene Mary's voice came over the PA system, and my opportunities to be funny were soon done for the day.

Sister Irene Mary matter-of-factly announced that President Kennedy had been injured in Dallas. As we all looked around at one another confused as to what the big deal was, I yelled that he had probably gotten a nosebleed just thinking about sitting in the cheap seats at the Army-Navy game. The class thought this was worthy of a giggle or two, but their laughter was soon interrupted when Sister Irene Mary once again turned on the PA system.

The minute we heard the crackle of the PA coming on, we sat still and did not utter a word. Sister Margaret, seated at her desk, did not have to tell us to pay attention when she raised her head and looked straight toward the rear of the classroom. This time Sister Irene Mary's voice was noticeably different; she said in a stern, monotone, "I am sorry to report that President Kennedy is dead."

People often say that everything slows down when you're in an automobile accident. Maybe that's also true when we hear shocking news, such as the assassination of a beloved president. I can still see Sister Margaret with her mouth wide open in shock and her head swinging backward, almost hitting the blackboard behind her desk. The girls were crying, and the boys didn't know what to do. No one seemed to be moving, but during those brief seconds on an otherwise quiet Friday afternoon, fifty or so thirteen-year-olds suddenly aged, if not matured, right before one another's eyes. We were completely unaware that an old world was ending as a new, uncertain, and scary world took its place.

—᯾—

After the initial shock wore off, if it ever really did, our class just sat there not knowing what to do or say. Sister Margaret suggested that we pray, and I guess we did, but for the life of me, I couldn't tell you what prayer was said.

Friday afternoons are notoriously slow, especially between the hours of two and three o'clock. It is believed by many in my class that the earth, at least the Bronx portion of it, drifts into a twilight zone where all movement ceases and humankind, at least the eighth grade portion of it, enters a state of suspended animation. It is thought that while in this state, our hearts stop beating and time comes to a crushing halt. Yet, on this particular Friday afternoon, time seemed to defy the laws of physics as we leapt forward to three o'clock in the blink of an eye. For no sooner had Sister Irene Mary uttered, "the president is dead" than Sister Margaret followed with the refrain "through

Christ our Lord, Amen," and we were walking down the stairs with our books and filing out of the building.

One of the girls suggested that we should go over to the church to pray for President Kennedy. I don't know if it was because we were especially religious or because we just didn't want to go home yet, but a bunch of us went into the church. It seemed like the right thing to do.

Later, the guys and I still had our regularly scheduled football game, but no one seemed too excited as we merely went through the motions. It wasn't until a little later that we were made aware just how deep our malaise ran.

There is an unwritten, though sacred, rule that states that all play stops with neither team being charged a time-out when a particularly interesting example of God's handiwork, as expressed in a rather appealing form of femininity, comes within viewing distance of the field. We had indeed become slaves to our newly acquired hormones. There were, in fact, two regularly scheduled biologically induced time-outs: one for K. Boff and the other for Stretch.

K. Boff was, how shall I say, healthy. Though Mike found her bordering on plump, PJ, Trent, and the rest of the players would gladly suffer the extra girth she bore. Her propensity for wearing skintight jeans and extremely tight sweaters delighted us sufficiently enough to break off play no matter how critical an impact it might have on the outcome of the game.

Stretch was another cause for *footballus interruptus*. Unlike K. Boff, Stretch was tall (hence her nickname Stretch) and slender; she was quite statuesque, really. Her overwhelming attributes, to which none could gainsay, were her legs. (Did I mention that I am trying to use all the vocab words we are studying for the COOP exam?) In furtherance of accentuating her God-given attributes, she took to wearing extremely short, red skirts accompanied by sheer, black stockings—the pièce de résistance. Well, you get the point.

Today, however, the game proceeded without female distractions. When PJ noted that we hadn't seen either of our expected sideline attractions, we all stopped what we were doing. When Trent chimed in and said that they had in fact passed by, but that we had kept playing without taking the time to pay attention, that's when we gave up on the game and decided to go home.

When I got home, my mother had the TV on, which was not like her, but given the day's events, I really wasn't surprised. Every station had something about the assassination. Whether it was the new president being sworn in on Air Force One or a discussion about the guy they arrested, Lee Harvey Oswald, every channel carried something about what had happened to President Kennedy.

Of course, there were those who thought the Russians or Cubans had done it, but it did appear that Oswald had pulled the trigger even if someone else put him up to it.

Saturday came and the nightmare that was yesterday persevered and took hold of the nation's spirit. Assassinations were something we read about in history books, not newspapers, and they were certainly not seen on TV. That, of course, was how it used to be, and we had no reason to believe that anything would ever be the way it used to be.

In addition to the unanswered questions that arose about the whos and whys of the assassination, there came reports that Sunday's football games would not be cancelled. Apparently, the National Football League reasoned that President Kennedy, being an avid football fan, would have wanted the games to proceed. Hearing this, all I could think about was what we had read the day before in the *Young Catholic Messenger* about President Kennedy going to the Army-Navy game. The dilemma the president had been facing as to which team to root for or where to sit seemed like a problem for a far less complicated world than the new one in which we now found ourselves.

School was cancelled for Monday, but Mass that Sunday was not. So I, along with six hundred other kids, arrived at the church at 9:45 a.m. for the 10:00 a.m. Mass. Father Toplisky, our music teacher, had us practicing the Credo prior to Mass. According to Father Tops, as we called him, the previous Sunday we had been a little slow and very flat, which is how I thought the Gregorian chant was supposed to sound.

Getting up for Mass on Sundays was hard enough, but having to sing like a monk in a monastery was a bit much to ask of teenagers, and it required a special type of motivation-Sister Emmaline.

All Father Tops had to do was utter her name, and even the most hardened miscreant, of which our class had quite a few, would chant a chant that would have put a smile on Pope Gregory's face despite the fact that he was still quite dead.

Having sung our hearts out, if not our immortal souls, we successfully got through the Mass and headed home for a nice Sunday breakfast.

The Sunday papers were filled with accounts of the assassination and the assassin. Only once before had I been so captivated by a news story, and not surprisingly, President Kennedy had played a role in it, too. Just about a year before, the Russians had put nuclear missiles in Cuba less than a hundred miles from the coast of Florida. The president ordered a naval blockade to keep the Russian supply ships out of Cuba, and it looked as though it was going to provoke World War III.

In school, we practiced putting our heads under our desks in case war broke out during the day. At night, my mother led the family in on-your-knees Rosaries accompanied by a splash of holy water when we went to bed. The night that the crisis came to a head, the air raid siren atop P.S. 47, our local public school, went off at 2:00 a.m. My entire family jumped out of bed, and my mother headed for the holy water. With the siren blaring and all of us wiping holy water out of our eyes, we awaited Armageddon. Fortunately, as we learned the following morning, Armageddon turned out to be an electrical short in the siren's wiring.

Anyway, President Kennedy stuck to his guns, so the Russians dropped their missiles and sanity was restored, however briefly. Now the president was dead, and I wondered what could possibly happen next. The answer to that question came much sooner than I could have imagined.

I was the first one in my family who could not remember a time before television. Although I do remember listening to some shows on radio, most of our entertainment revolved around the TV. My mother often complained that I didn't read enough. When I protested that I was an avid reader, she replied that Superman comics did not count. She had all sorts of sayings and theories regarding life and its mysteries thanks to her own mother and the good teachers of County Sligo in Ireland. One of my favorites of her sayings is "Too much of anything is good for nothing," which she recited at least once a day when she turned off the television set.

On this particular Sunday, we had not yet reached that portion of the TV viewing day, so as I caught up on my reading of *Moon Mullins* and *Gasoline Alley* in the Sunday comics, I was able to witness an event of immense historical and cultural significance.

Lee Harvey Oswald was being transferred somewhere, and TV viewers were going to get a glimpse of America's newest villain. Just as Oswald appeared on the screen, when he was entering a room of wall-to-wall cops, some fat guy in a fedora came out of nowhere, pulled out a gun, and shot Oswald dead. This was a TV first: live murder, coast to coast in brilliant black and white.

Live murder—as incongruous a juxtaposition of words as you could imagine, yet even more incongruous was the apparent ease with which one assassin became the victim of another.

Seconds later I heard a voice say, "Too much of anything is good for nothing." Only this time the voice was my own, as was the hand turning off the television.

CHAPTER 2

THEN THERE'S CHRISTMAS

Thanksgiving came and went without much ado. Turkey was eaten, and Green Bay played Detroit in football: life goes on.

Finally, Friday had come, and with it, the Christmas holiday season began. This was going to be a great day for football, and maybe I would get over to Macy's to see them set up the trains in preparation for Christmas. There was no doubt that Christmas was certainly in the air.

I was walking to Hoch's candy store with the guys after our football game when we came upon Laura and Kathy. It looked as though the two of them were heading to Laura's house. I was kind of leery of saying anything to them, as I still hadn't spoken to Kathy yet, but Mike urged me to follow them, so I took my chances.

The two of us double-timed it and caught up to them.

"Hey, what say we hang out a bit?" Mike offered.

Laura had a self-satisfied look, as though she was in control of the civilized world, when she said, "Sorry, boys, but we have to get ready for the roller skating trip tonight."

"What roller skating trip?" I asked, not really wanting to find out.

"Father Dolan and Father Gorman are taking the altar boys, and they asked us to go along to keep them company."

I hate altar boys! I can't tell you how many times my mother sang the praises of my brother Johnnie for being an altar boy. He was on the altar at five in the morning on school days and even during summer vacation.

My brother Michael and I waged a contest to see who could roll their eyes the most without getting caught every time she brought up Saint Johnny of the Cross. I think that is the reason why we never became altar boys. Well, to be honest, I did try out for the altar boys back in the fifth grade, but Father Dolan was a bit too rough back then, and he scared the bejesus out of me, so I soon quit. Not having to memorize the Confiteor in Latin only made quitting sweeter.

Not only did I have to live with my altar boy failure; now I would have to face the fact that some altar boy would be skating with my girl—well, once I finally got around to asking her to be my girl.

Mike and I left the girls and walked to the corner. "So whaddya want to do?" asked Mike.

"I don't know; go home I guess," I replied.

"Hey, I have an idea. Let's meet up tonight around six thirty, and we can at least walk them to the school."

"Are you sure you want to run the risk of looking pathetic when they get on the bus?" I asked.

"Listen, buddy boy, we can make this work in our favor; just trust Mikey."

So, later that evening, there I was walking down Leland with Mike and wondering if we were doing the right thing. But just as we arrived at the corner of Gleason and Thieriot, who do we see coming right up Thieriot Avenue heading our way but Laura and Kathy all dolled up and ready to go. I tried to ignore the fact that they were ready to go with some other guys.

"Good evening, ladies, may I say you look simply ludicrous tonight," Mike said as the girls moved closer to us while shaking their heads at Mike's joke. "Mr. Newell here thought it would be a good idea if we walked you to the school."

"I did? I mean, yes, of course, we want to make sure you get there safe and sound."

Laura had a smirk on her face, and I couldn't tell what Kathy was thinking. I never knew what she was thinking, and I am getting tired of that let me tell you.

We did get to walk them to the school, nonetheless. Mike and I were funny and charming, and by the time we got to the schoolyard, where a big yellow school bus was idling, Laura and Kathy were laughing and having a good time with us, but then they had to leave. All I could think was that we had warmed them up for two other guys.

Laura got on the bus first, followed by Kathy. All of a sudden, Father Dolan came out of the bus and saw Mike and me. "Hey, Newell, O'Connor, what are you doing?"

"Nothing, Father, we just walked Laura and Kathy here."

"Well go home and put nice pants on. You can't wear dungarees at the skating rink," he said.

Mike and I looked at each other and immediately started to run home. Father Dolan shouted after us, "Don't give your mothers a stroke. Take your time. We'll wait."

As we ran home, Mike asked, "What just happened?"

"I don't know. Maybe he thought we were altar boys."

Ten minutes later, we met outside Mike's building and ran to the school. To our great relief, the bus was still there. We scooted up the steps, and to our great shock and joy, Laura and Kathy were sitting in separate seats, and both motioned us to sit next to them—me with Kathy and Mike with Laura. I felt like praying.

This bus ride turned out to be even better than the time we went on a trip to a carnival up in Nanuet. On that trip, I was able to sit next to Laura, and we had a good laugh, so I knew she would report back to Kathy that I was witty and charming. Maybe she really had done that, because here I was sitting next to Kathy. I guessed now would be a good time to actually speak to her.

Anybody who knows me knows I can talk. I come from a long line of talkers. There is not a shy one in our family, and I have never had a problem competing in the talking department. Some say I love to hear myself talk. I don't deny it. But here I was sitting next to a girl I had been dreaming about for three months, and I was coming up empty.

Kathy must have read my mind because she started talking first. "So, do you know how to roller skate?"

"Oh yeah, I'm a pretty good skater; in fact, I have my own skates and all."

"You do? Where are they?"

"Well, it was all I could do to get my pants on."

This made her laugh uncontrollably. I was home free! From that moment on, we had a great night. I'm not sure she knew exactly how great it was, but it was a great night.

When we got to the rink, we immediately put our skates on and started skating. Mike and I were following the girls, but then we lost them. A few minutes later, they caught up with us from the back and skated with us hand in hand. Let me repeat that: HAND IN HAND. There I was skating and holding hands with Kathy. I don't know how I didn't pass out.

After a few minutes of holding hands, however, I was wishing I had passed out. Never in my wildest dreams would I have ever imagined that my hand could sweat as much as it was now sweating. This was embarrassing. Finally, the two of us let go, and we both wiped our hands on our pants and laughed. Even sweating was no sweat tonight. *Thank you, God,* I prayed inwardly.

We sat and had a soda with Mike and Laura, and then we skated some more, and before I knew it, we were getting back on the bus to go home. I wanted Kathy to know how I felt about her. Of course, I couldn't tell her, but it was obvious, wasn't it? So I figured there was no sense saying anything more about it. Mike, on the other hand, was all for spilling his guts, and was soon doing just that in the seat in front of us. It must have worked, because by the time we were getting off the bus, he and Laura were going out.

I still didn't feel the need. It was obvious how I felt, wasn't it?

Christmas in the city is always something special. Back then in the Bronx, the trappings of Christmas overwhelmed our senses. The sights and smells of Christmas were everywhere. All along Metropolitan Avenue, trees and lights beckoned Christmas shoppers to Macy's, the Five and Ten and all the other stores in Parkchester.

At the Oval, the fountains of summer gave way to winter wonderland houses bedecked and bedazzled in red and green lights and artificial snow. The Dollar Savings Bank on the Circle had a set of trains set up in the lobby and the Santa Claus House, which had recently been a stack of lumber in front of the Loew's American, was now fully constructed and inhabited by a right jolly old elf. Even after a national tragedy and the uncertainty that it engendered, Christmastime prevailed, and it was hard not to be caught up in the spirit of it all.

The most obvious sign that Christmastime had arrived, however, was the bundle of Christmas trees stacked at the entrance of every gin mill in our neighborhood. By no means could they have been mistaken by anyone for ordinary Christmas trees, for these were genuine XMAS trees. Though most passersby may have ignored this distinction, it glared out as a brazen sign of ignominy and calumny to one Michael A. Newell, my father.

My dad viewed the use of XMAS as blasphemy and un-American, and no tree would ever enter our house if it stood under such a sign of denigration and disrespect. He didn't like XMAS.

It was all we could do to persuade him to buy a tree at another establishment, so sure was he that it would no doubt employ such a pagan sign. For this reason, my brother Michael would carry his own sign to the next closest gin mill selling trees and place it upon the tree we had pre-selected.

My father's reluctance to buy an XMAS tree extended to Christmas trees as well, as the possibility of a fire in the house was his one and only concern. This was easy to understand, as the great post-holiday sport on our block was the annual gathering of the neighborhood Christmas trees and assembling them in a pyre in the lot adjoining our apartment building. Once put afire, the height of the resulting inferno and the sweet smell of pine was a reminder of what excellent kindling Christmas trees make.

Ignoring these Yuletide misgivings and wishing to provide a bountiful Christmas for his family, my father relented, and on Christmas Eve, he purchased an eight-foot, genuine Douglas Fir Christmas, not to be confused with XMAS, tree.

Michael and I carried it home and up the two flights of stairs to Apartment 6, our humble abode. No sooner had we cut the ropes holding the branches than the phone rang. It was our brother Johnny. He was working a second job at Macy's and wanted to speak to our father.

Michael and I continued to prepare the tree for decorating. As we were about to jam the tree into the stand, my father gave a shout of joy and told us to open the window. Michael and I reacted with a coordinated, two-part harmony of, "Huh?"

My father looked at us like we were two knuckleheads who couldn't understand the English language. He then explained with a Saint Nick-like glee that Johnny had bought us an artificial tree, so we could now throw out this real, beautiful, smells-like-Christmas Douglas fir Christmas tree. In a later age, Michael and I would have texted WTF. But in 1963, we just stood there dumbfounded.

My father was still not impressed with the alacrity with which we grasped the situation; he ignored our delay and told Michael to go downstairs to make sure no one was hit with our tree when we threw it out the window. Now it was getting serious.

Despite our failure to understand or act accordingly, the tree was deposited out the window onto Leland Avenue without further incident. Michael assigned it to the lot for a fire that was more than a week away, and then he came back upstairs.

Michael, ever the optimist, said, "Some of those trees they have in Macy's are pretty nice, so maybe it won't be so bad."

We still had all our decorations and lights, and with a little garland, this tree would turn out okay—at least that was what we told ourselves.

So, to the backdrop of Bing Crosby singing with the Andrews Sisters and my mother baking in the kitchen, we rebounded and got back into the Christmas spirit. Then the bell rang and Johnny was home. As soon as my father heard the bell, he immediately went to the TV, on top of which our Nativity was in its usual place, and started clearing it off. Now what?

Something was wrong, and we were not relieved when we saw Johnny enter the living room with a small box tucked under his arm.

With "Mele Kelikimaka" echoing in our heads, Johnny opened the box and pulled out a white dwarf tree with red and green lights embedded in the branches, and he perched it on top of the television. That was it: no tinsel, no balls, and no Angie the Christmas tree angel. You couldn't put anything on this tree if you wanted to. The only thing you could do was plug it in and let yourself bathe in its holiday charm.

So, as the best Christmas tree we had ever had lay as refuse in the lot awaiting a match, this poor excuse for a shrub sought to shine a light for the winter solstice.

Since it was still early in the evening, Michael and I went out for a quickie. Now for adults this might mean a drink of holiday cheer in the Yolk, the alternate name for Pete's bar. For Michael and me, a quickie represented a different type of mood-altering activity. For us, a visit to Macy's train layout was just what we needed, as trains were as much a part of Christmas as singing carols or roasting chestnuts by the glow of a red light bulb in our cardboard fireplace.

Despite having several sets of Lionel trains already, we always dreamed about getting more. So now, our Lionel dream therapy would provide the solace in our time of Christmas tree remorse.

Christmas day came, and our attention was drawn to other things. Johnny and my sisters, Maureen and Barbara, came over with their spouses and kids so there was too big a crowd around the dinner table, which was set up in the living room, to notice what a ridiculous tree we had. No one even noticed how every now and then Michael and I looked at each other and shook our heads in disbelief. Of one thing I was certain: I would not be unhappy when we took the tree down this year.

Christmas week was always one of the best times of the entire year. It rivaled the first week of summer vacation. The only problem was that families often got in the way, and instead of playing football or just hanging out, the guys were often dragged off to Aunt Catherine's, Uncle Sonny's, or any of the myriad relatives we all had populating the environs of the Bronx.

One of the annual traditions in my family was my brother Johnny treating my mother and I to lunch at Luchow's down on Fourteenth Street. They always had a beautiful Christmas tree, and they made a goulash that was worth the long ride on the 6 train. Each year my mother and I would traipse downtown and have a great meal with my brother and maybe do a little shopping. Despite being a former altar boy and a saint, Johnny was still a great brother. This year, though, there was a problem.

Going anywhere with your mother when you were twelve or eleven was fine. Now, however, being thirteen, I was getting a little old to be dragged anywhere by my mother as though I was still a kid or something. The good news was that Johnny said nothing about Luchow's at this year's Christmas dinner. He had other plans.

On the Monday after Christmas, my mother dropped a bombshell. It seemed that good old Johnny had given us tickets to Radio City. My mother was all excited when she told me that we would be going the following day. We would see the tree in Rockefeller Center (which we always did), and maybe we would go to lunch before going to Radio City. I was dying. I had already made plans with Mike, PJ, and Trent to go downtown, and we were planning to meet up with the girls. How was I going to get out of this one?

I was convinced my mother had supernatural powers. One of her cousins used to bring her friends over, and my mother would read their tealeaves. She was always going on about some crazy story that she had heard back in Sligo. Her stories often sounded as though Edgar Allen Poe had written them. My favorite was the girl who told her sister to drop dead, and the sister dropped dead right there and then. The other sister went insane. Is that like something on *The Twilight Zone* or what? That's why, when my mother got that look, I knew she was on to me.

I knew the jig was up, so I didn't do or say anything suspicious until the next day, just a few hours before we were set to leave. I got out of bed and made a face as though I was in pain. I swear to God, I think she was already shaking her head thinking what a lummox I was.

She said, "What's the matter? Are you not feeling well?"

Right on cue, I replied, "My stomach is a little upset."

"Ah, well, maybe we shouldn't be traipsing off downtown today, then."

You know, it was akin to being in the confessional with Father Gorman; she saw right through me, but she was cool about it. I was too. I didn't jump at the open door she had laid out for me, but I got dressed, and we both sat down to a little breakfast. All the while, those Irish eyes of hers looked deep into my immortal soul.

What could I do? This was the same woman who told me she would pounce on the principal of St. Helena's High School in case I really did blow the COOP exam and failed to get into a Catholic high school. I couldn't break her heart and tell her I would rather go with my friends. What's worse, she knew damn well I didn't have the stomach for it either.

So there I was having a piece of her Irish soda bread and realizing I was going to Radio City with my mother after all. Knowing the situation, she gave me an opening.

"Maybe you're feeling a little bit better and you can try going to the show."

"Yeah, I think I can go."

The funny thing was that Lizzie McHugh knew me better than I knew myself. We got on the 6 train and immediately had a great time. No one enjoyed people watching more than my mother did. I saw a woman who had enough makeup on to doll up all the Radio City Rockettes, who we would be seeing in just a few hours. My mother noticed her too, and we gave a little nod to each other as we shared our silent joke, and then we laughed like crazy when we changed trains at 125th Street.

Christmas in the city was always something to behold. As we walked across 59th Street toward Fifth Avenue, we took in all the sights. Once on Fifth, the fun really began. We loved to visit 666 Fifth Avenue, where my sister Barbara worked, because they always displayed huge snowflakes on the upper level of the building that were truly spectacular. Then we stopped off at Tiffany's, and I promised my mom that I would get her a diamond ring one day to go with the fur stole I would also buy for her. While we were in the vicinity, we went to FAO Schwartz and saw what the rich kids got for Christmas.

Then, my mother, making sure I didn't forget what Christmas was all about, made us turn into St. Patrick's for a little prayer and to see the manger. Having acknowledged the season, we headed to the tree in Rockefeller Center. Every year the tree in Rockefeller Center is the focal point of the holiday as celebrated by New Yorkers. I don't know anyone who hasn't made the pilgrimage downtown at least once in his or her life. This year's was as magnificent as any I had ever seen. My mother thought so too, though she seemed to be looking at me more than the tree.

I caught her looking and just nodded. We both knew this was going to be a special day, and any hesitation I had about going out with my mother was a far distant memory that I would never own up to.

I couldn't imagine how the day could get better, but it did. Fortunately, the line to get into Radio City was not that long, especially since we had our tickets already. Good old Johnny had come through as always. (Michael and I had gotten over the Christmas tree affair.) No sooner had we gotten in line than we were ushered to our seats. Ours were in the mezzanine, which was great because we were just high enough that we wouldn't have a fat woman with a big hat blocking our view, but we could still see the Rockettes's legs glowing in the dark.

Before the Rockettes and the Nativity pageant, there was always a movie. The program indicated that it would be *Charade* with Audrey Hepburn and Cary Grant. I just wanted to see the Rockettes, but good fortune was looking out for me again.

I'm not sure if it was because I was sitting in Radio City at Christmastime or because I was there with my mother, but *Charade* turned out to be the best movie I had ever seen. I would have sat through that movie three times in a row, which is what my mother and I did when we saw *Snow White* at the Loew's Paradise.

If Audrey Hepburn isn't the most beautiful woman in the world, I don't know who is, and who is cooler than Cary Grant? After watching *Charade,* I forgot all about the Rockettes. In fact, as the credits ended and I got up to leave, my mother reminded me about the Rockettes and the Nativity. I could see her laughing to herself as she dragged me back down to my seat. She knew.

The Rockettes were great, the Nativity was as spectacular as advertised, and as we headed to the Automat for a late lunch, I realized that my mother and I had enjoyed a day together that I would remember even as an old man.

CHAPTER 3

FOR ALL YOU BOYS AND GIRLS

January in the Bronx was not especially pleasant, unless of course we had enough snow to get a snow day or two out of it. However, this January promised to be different. "I Want to Hold Your Hand," "Please Please Me," and "She Loves You" proved too much for the post-holiday blues and the bleak New York winter weather. Beatlemania snatched us out of our despair brought on by the cold and the lingering darkness of the Kennedy assassination.

What started as a late-night one-time airing of "I Want to Hold Your Hand" on Music Radio WABC back in November had, by January, transformed into a phenomenon and a revolution that was only beginning to affect American youth culture. Each of the three New York rock-and-roll radio stations tried to outdo one another by claiming to be the official Beatle radio station. Murray the K on WINS called himself the Fifth Beatle while Cousin Brucie and Scot Muni on WABC and the Good Guys on WMCA refused to be outdone in the promotion department. Regardless of whom you listened to, a Beatle song was heard every five minutes.

Unlike most songs that required a certain familiarity before they were able to exert their primitive, pagan hypnotic spell over me, "I Want to Hold Your Hand" had me the first time I heard it. I was hooked on the Beatles from the first chord. Even on my eight-transistor radio, the electric intensity that the Beatles generated brought me to an ethereal realm of imaginary guitars and fanatical girls who couldn't get enough of my singing and playing.

The excitement that the Beatles engendered made it hard to believe that only a few short months ago our president had been shot dead, as had his assassin. Even as our nation continued to struggle with the hows, whys, and whos of this tragedy, these four guys from Liverpool, England, helped us get through our grief. In fact, maybe that's all we really needed—someone to hold our hand. As America found itself akin to a lost child in a new and frightening world, we looked for comfort and reassurance. Enter John, Paul, George, and Ringo.

The Beatles yeah, yeah, yeahed their way into our hearts and even into our immortal souls, though we didn't tell that to Sister Margaret or Monsignor Hart.

Of course, there were the usual doubters. Those were mainly the older generation—eighteen- to twenty-year-olds who clung to memories conceived in jukeboxes and born at sock hops and rock-and-roll shows where they danced with their little darlins and doo-wopped and rama-lama-ding-donged to the music of the *Del-Vikings* and *The Flamingos*. These groups, it should be noted, were still vital to us younger enthusiasts, their songs provided the very much-desired slow dance opportunities at our Friday night parties and perhaps the greatest rock and roll group of all time, *Dion and The Belmonts*, were Bronx Boys after all.

Nevertheless, as February replaced January, and the Beatles stormed into America and onto *The Ed Sullivan Show*, the D A succumbed to the Mop Top, and music would never be heard quite the same way again.

When the Beatles landed at Idlewild Airport—I mean Kennedy Airport—it seemed that every newspaper, television, and radio station had reporters ready to greet them. That night I read in the *Journal American* that John Lennon was known as the "sexy" Beatle. I made sure to hide this reference from my mother because I knew that sex was something my parents frowned upon, as my two brothers and two sisters could confirm.

My mother was a devotee of rock and roll. She loved listening to the Everly Brothers and Buddy Holly, her favorite performers. She was excited to see me reading the newspaper, especially the news section instead of sports or the comics.

She was also happy that I was getting interested in Irish culture; she was convinced that John Lennon and Paul McCartney were two nice Irish lads. When I cautiously tried to tell her that they were actually English lads from Liverpool, she scoffed at my suggestion and replied, "Luv, there are more Irish in Liverpool than there are in Dublin."

Anyway, neither my mother nor my father complained when I played "I Want to Hold Your Hand" so often you could almost hear the flip side "I Saw Her Standing There," at the same time.

Finally, the Sunday we had all been waiting for arrived, and we were all bursting with excitement. Even the die-hard doo-woppers had gotten into it, perhaps sensing the end of their era. The radio stations kept up their competition for our attention, and you couldn't dial in a station without hearing a Beatles song.

It was now eight o'clock at night, and *The Ed Sullivan Show* came into view on our twenty-three-inch, black-and-white television screen. I did not worry about whether I had done my homework. This was probably the first, and only, time that watching Ed Sullivan did not result in that horrible feeling of undone homework. Instead, my only anxiety revolved around which songs the Beatles would sing. I was just about ready to jump off the couch. Fortunately, Mr. Sullivan did not torture us too long, and he shouted out, "The Beatles!" almost as soon as he started talking.

The Kennedy assassination was the first event I experienced that I know I will always remember where I was and what I was doing when I heard the news. Now, I had something else to add to the list. When the Beatles came into view and Paul started singing the first line of "All My Loving" and all the girls in the audience began screaming, crying, and fainting, I knew I would never forget what I saw, heard, or felt that night.

I feared that our poor twenty-three-inch television set could not contain the electricity and excitement that the Beatles were generating. Our living room seemed to be encased in a sphere of sonic energy that could repel assassins and Dien Bien Phus, atom bombs and final exams. Within this sphere, you could scream for joy and not from terror. The distinction between sensual enjoyment and sexual fulfillment was for a moment obscured if not totally eliminated. (Puberty really does affect your choice of metaphors.)

As tired as I was after a night like no other night I'd ever had, and after staying up listening to the radio in bed, it was not hard getting up for school the next morning. I couldn't wait to talk to everyone about what we had seen and heard. Beatles cards were bought and Beatles songs were sung, and I actually toyed with the idea of buying a Beatles wig. Few doubted that we were witnessing something uniquely powerful. This was not a one-time thing. Ed Sullivan saw to that, as he had the Beatles on his show again next Sunday and the one after that.

Mike had a song magazine that had all the words to this week's top ten, but we were only interested in the Beatles songs. At first glance, the lyrics seemed typical of rock and roll songs. They were far from poetic, although they did seem to rhyme. But that didn't matter. Just reading the lyrics to these songs made me smile, and when I played their records, I just had to sing along, and sitting was out of the question.

There was one problem, however. Ordinarily no one particularly cared what your favorite song was or who your favorite singer was. Music wasn't baseball. Now, if you wanted to have something in common with certain females of the attractive persuasion, you had better have done your homework. It was clear, too, that you had to make a decision. No way would a blanket endorsement of the Fab Four and their songs suffice. It was far better to choose incorrectly than not to choose at all.

Nor was consistency a prerequisite. For example, it was quite acceptable to pick "Till There Was You" as your favorite song, which was sung by Paul, and then select Ringo as your favorite Beatle, which is exactly what I did. It did not matter that my real choices were "I Want to Hold Your Hand" and John. What mattered is what I told everyone. My decision to go public with "Till There Was You" and Ringo was based on the following logic.

"Till There Was You" was a romantic, lovey-dovey type of song, which would reveal how the woman of my dreams was necessary for me to enjoy all of life's pleasures. Selecting Ringo illustrated my sensitive side and showed that there was more to me than a guy looking for a pretty face. This strategy could not fail in helping me get on the good side of the ladies. But as luck would have it, the one young lady who was the target of my Beatlemaniacal machinations was the one girl at Blessed Sacrament School who did not like the Beatles.

There was nothing else to do but rely on my fallback plan: charm and good looks.

It was going to be a very long, lonely winter.

As it turned out, the winter didn't seem that long, and it wasn't especially lonely. Eighth grade continued to be such a gas that school days were almost as much fun as the weekends. Maybe it was the realization that grammar school was coming to an end. That meant I wouldn't be going to Blessed Sacrament for too much longer, and I wouldn't see most of my classmates again, so our time together was going to be special. Despite the fact that most of us would attend a Catholic high school, there were so many different schools all over the city to choose from that it was unlikely we would all be going to the same one. Anyhow, the last six months at Blessed Sacrament would be memorable.

The intensity of the work diminished once we had taken the hated COOP exam. We had to take this test in order to qualify for a Catholic high school. Failure to qualify would be a fate worse than death, so Rosaries and Novenas were said by one and all. I really prayed, and even my mother took note.

This test was unlike any test we had ever taken. We didn't write the answers to the questions on a sheet of loose-leaf paper or in one of those blue test booklets they gave us for midterms and finals. For this test, we had to read the question in a booklet and make a mark on a separate answer sheet. We had to use a number two pencil, and we had to make the mark neatly inside a circle. Sister Margaret went on and on about how we had to do this neatly without erasing or leaving stray marks, or else the answer would be marked as wrong. She kept looking at me when she said this. I blame her for what happened.

The day of the test came, and I was psyched. I flew through the questions, and I was doing an excellent job of not making a mess of my answer sheet until I came to the last page. According to the test booklet, I only had ten questions to finish, but for some reason I had twenty circles on my answer sheet. I then noticed that I was about to put the answer to question ninety-one in the answer for question eighty-one. As my father was often heard saying, my mind erupted with *Jesus, Mary, and Joseph!*

After realizing my mistake, I went back and found that at question sixty-one, I must have turned two pages at once, so I was really answering question seventy-one and putting that answer and all the ones that followed in the wrong circle. I now had to go back, erase, and redo the last forty questions in fifteen minutes!

By the time I finished, my answer sheet was a mess. Neatness was never one of my strengths, but this test was a disaster to look at. All I could remember was seeing Sister Margaret's face as she looked at me when talking about the serious consequences for erasing on this test. Because a computer would be "reading" the test instead of a human, what it couldn't read would be marked wrong. I was dead. My test was a mess, and so was my life. There was no way I was ever going to get into a Catholic high school now.

In history, we read about a group called the Luddites who were against all the modern technology being developed during the Industrial Revolution. At the time, I thought they were barbarians for trying to resist progress. Now, I was looking to organize a Bronx chapter.

My trepidation, however, was for naught as I was accepted to each of the four high schools that I had listed as my preferences, and Sister Margaret could rest easy once again and allow me to as well.

It wasn't that we didn't like Protestants or were afraid of them. It was just that there weren't that many of them in our neighborhood. We heard they didn't have Latin hymns, and it was common knowledge that if you went to a Protestant Mass, you would surely be struck dead, but I didn't believe that. To be honest, though, I didn't take any chances.

Jewish kids, on the other hand, were part of our neighborhood clan, and the only differences we noted was that they went to church on Saturdays and had to attend Hebrew classes. Sure, we learned about what happened in the World War II, and I could never understand why there was so much persecution of Jewish people in Christian countries. After all, Jesus was Jewish, and it was his grandmother, Saint Anne, who had helped me overcome my test-taking blunder and gotten me into a Catholic high school. How could you be an anti-Semite and pray to a Jewish grandmother?

While we took note of differences, I don't think we did it to be mean. It was more like we were spectators or enthusiasts who rooted for our team. It was like arguing over Mickey, Willie, and the Duke, but just a little bit harder to change your allegiance.

My friends ran the ethnic gamut. Mike's family came from County Cork, Ireland, PJ's from County Mayo, also in Ireland, and Trent and Freddie's families hailed from "County" Sicily in Italy. Okay, so we weren't exactly a United Nations, but in addition to Irish and Italians, our group consisted of Polish and German guys and a few whose country of origin, some might say planet of origin, could not be readily identified. Regardless of where our parents came from, our loyalties were to one another and our neighborhood.

The winds of crisis would often test our tensile strength of friendship, and on at least one occasion, I was the one ensnared in its vortex. When that happened, my comrades-in-arms came to the rescue.

On an otherwise typical afternoon while playing football, a busted play transformed my erstwhile cannon of a football-throwing arm into a crude weapon of mayhem and destruction. The play was for Mike to do a down-and-out behind the '63 Chevy Impala, which, if completed, would have been a ten-yard gain. Mike read a blitz, faked the down-and-out, and headed downfield for a bomb. Usually Mike and I were in sync, and our success in this area had been legendary, at least on Leland and Thieriot Avenues.

However, on this particular day, I missed the sign. So instead of a simple pump fake and a lofty bomb down the center of the street, I threw a bullet to the original target. Instead of a completed pass and a first down, I hit the taillight of the '63 Chevy Impala causing the taillight to shatter. This was a first for me. I had never broken so much as a window—well, except for the one when I was a kid back in sixth grade. Then there was the time I threw a pass that hit a telephone line draped across the street, but anyone could have done that. This time, however, it was serious. There would be repercussions.

For one thing, the car belonged to Laura's father, and I had to remain in good standing with Laura if I ever was to have a chance with Kathy. Even with that, I could have run away and hoped that Laura's father would think that a car trying to squeeze in behind him while parking had broken the light. But as luck would have it, Fran, the town crier, was watching us play and ran up to Laura's house before the last shard of glass hit the street. Now I had to come up with the money to pay for the taillight, which would cost eleven dollars and seventy-five cents, as Laura was only too happy to inform me the next day.

Where would I ever get such a large sum of money? The concept of an allowance had not yet been adopted on Leland Avenue, at least not in 1261 Apartment 6. No, there was no reserve fund to access in my hour of need. Of course, there was Aunt Catherine, but she had just spotted me her annual twenty bucks at Christmas, and that was long since spent. Easter was still a few months away, so Aunt Catherine would not come to the rescue. Neither was I considered an expense item on the Newell family budget. I came under the miscellaneous, ad hoc category, which required a written requisition in triplicate, replete with explanations and countersigned by both parents. I now knew what the saying "left out to dry" meant, at least until my friends rallied to my support.

Errands were run, soda bottles were returned, and sidewalks were shoveled until I was walking around with pockets bulging with coinage of various denominations. In just a week's time, our group effort had collected ten dollars and seventy-five cents. However, I was still a buck short, and the deadline was tomorrow. There was no way I could ever come up with such a sum in one day's time. It was a valiant effort, but I was coming up short.

So there I was with Mike and Trent standing on the corner of Gleason and Thieriot Avenues trying to come up with some sort of a plan when Freddie and PJ came bopping down the street. We must have looked like a bunch of sad sacks because Freddie asked, "Who died?"

Actually, at this time I used to call him Alfred because that is what was stitched on his jacket. Now Alfred was a kid we all knew, but he hadn't started hanging around with us yet. He was a good guy who lived on the other side of Westchester Avenue, which was literally the other side of the tracks—old trolley car tracks actually—except we were the ones who lived on the other side of the tracks sociologically speaking. I told him what my problem was, and he quickly went into his pocket and dug out a buck; he handed it to me and asked if it would help.

I looked down at my hand and I did not recognize it at first. It wasn't shiny or metallic, but rather, it consisted of a paper-like substance, and it had the words Silver Certificate written over a picture of George Washington. I just couldn't understand what was happening. It was just amazing to think that he was giving me a dollar. I asked him, "What is this?"

He replied, "I think it's a dollar." Here he was just someone I knew by sight, and he was giving me a dollar and saving my immortal soul, not to mention my all too mortal ass.

I asked again, "What is this?" Trent tried to explain this time, Mike clarified it, and PJ suggested I get right over to Laura's house to pay off my debt before Freddie changed his mind. Never noted for my speed, I nonetheless ran like a deer and otherwise made tracks to Laura's house.

As I began the long climb up her stairs, I was startled by the sudden appearance of Laura's mother in the doorway. I had been dreading this confrontation for a week now, so I was anxious to get it over with. I just wanted to pay the money I owed and get the hell out of there. But it was not going to happen that way.

I was just about to tell her that I had all the money, but she wouldn't let me get a word out. She let me know how disappointed she was because I hadn't come to her first thing. When I explained that I knew loudmouth Fran had ratted me out before I knew what had happened, it sounded as lame an excuse to me as it did to her. I realized I had messed up, and I apologized. I told her I had the money, and that's when it got crazy.

I started pulling the money out of my pockets when she said, "That's okay—hearing you say sorry was enough."

I couldn't believe it. I was off the hook; I was now stuck with eleven dollars and seventy-five cents to boot. My reception committee waited for me on the corner. No one understood why I was fretting about having the money. I told them that I didn't know who had given me what except for Freddie. But Freddie wouldn't even consider taking his buck back, and such loyalty and unselfishness made him a fellow traveler for life.

What was I going to do with the money?

Well, my finance committee had the answer. The entire sum of eleven dollars and seventy-five cents would go to Jeannie to fund our Friday night soirees in her parent's basement. Eleven dollars and seventy-five cents would keep us in chips and soda for many a Friday night, and maybe even a record or two.

Later on that night, while reveling in my eleventh-hour acquittal, I had my first attack of adulthood. I really appreciated my narrow escape, but more important than getting out of a jam was how it had been achieved. Even though their money had proven unnecessary for my salvation, my friends had come through for me. I realized my good fortune in having friends the like of which enter your life very seldom and in limited number.

It was at this moment that I knew that these characters would be with me for life. Their life stories and mine would have overlapping chapters and intersecting themes and subplots. Together we would produce a catalogue of life's experiences by which all future data would be processed, evaluated, and applied when appropriate. Together we would rejoice our accomplishments and trivialize our failures. But for the moment, these adult sentiments of lifelong camaraderie needed to give way to pubescent lusts and teenaged cravings, because it was Friday night and time for Jeannie's first party of the season.

Jeannie lived with her parents and two little brothers in a private house, which in comparison to my two-bedroom apartment was palatial in size. Her parents were terrific. Their sole mission in life was to insure that their children had a safe home, and they allowed us to join them weekly for the ride. Every Friday night Jeannie's parents opened their home for our benefit so that we could hang out and listen to records, dance a little, and maybe have a soda or two. Never once did they ask us to lower the music or our voices, and believe me, they often had every reason to. They actually seemed happy to see us!

Since it was common practice for us to chip in for snacks and soda, the unanticipated donation from the Committee to Save Jimmy's Hiney was a welcomed event. We ate and drank like kings and queens. We were even able to buy a few records. I gave Jeannie and Rosemary the money, and they bought the records while the guys procured the food. This proved to be a strategic error that we lived to regret.

Although we all loved loud and fast songs, this variety of record was not conducive to our overwhelming desire to dance as closely as humanly possible with our fellow teenagers of the feminine gender. For myself, I was never quite sure if this animal urge was motivated by primal sexual urges or by the equally primal motivation to avoid making an ass of myself in public. Fast dancing was not something that came easy to me. To be honest, it didn't come at all.

Most of the guys felt the same way except for Mike, who always had a little more rhythm than the rest of us. Trent thought this was because Mike used to live in the projects. But even Mike preferred slow dancing, and he was always eager to share the nickname that the girls had given him (although he actually made it up). "They call me Coffee because my grind is so fine." Of course, this was never said in the girls' presence, but we always had a good laugh, nonetheless.

Not wishing to be outdone, I took advantage of the fact that there were often more girls than there were boys at our parties, so I would dance with two at one time. On this particular Friday night, Laura, who was dancing with Mike while I was dancing with Kathy and Theresa, turned to PJ and Trent and said, "We know about the coffee man here, and old two-timer over there, but what's your deal?"

To which I chimed in, "They have no deal; they just dance with each other." PJ and Trent got the last laugh, though, as they started dancing with Kathy and Theresa.

PJ lost no time and shouted out, "Hey, Nude, whaddya gonna do now?"

Like the second half of a comedy team, Trent responded, "He's used to doing things by himself." For whatever reason, all the boys thought that was pretty funny, but the girls just shook their heads in dismay. It didn't matter as far as I was concerned. This was a great night.

I then went over to the record player and loaded up some 45s to continue the party. The girls had bought "Twist and Shout," "Tell Me," and "Needles and Pins." Now we were in full swing, and it was only eight thirty, so we had more than an hour left to sing and dance.

Finally, Jeannie got some of her slow songs out, and we were home free. I even renewed my dance with Kathy. I thought this was pretty funny. I actually had danced with her twice, if only for a brief moment, but I hadn't had a conversation since the night we went skating other than when I asked, "Would you like to dance?" Well, that is what I intended to say, but it probably sounded more like, "Woof ya lie ta dan?" Kathy's pretty smart, so she was able to figure it out, but I am not so sure she could figure me out, or if she even wanted to figure me out.

I don't know what it was, but I always became tongue-tied around her, and I invariably said something stupid or completely unintelligible. Now, not only was I unable to talk, but I also had sweaty palms again. I mean, who sweats from their palms anyway—maybe bowlers? I wished I had those air-blowing things they have at the bowling alley 'cause I sure could have used them. She was probably thinking I had some kind of condition. I felt that I was sinking fast, so I did what I always try to do: act the clown.

I started trying to imitate Tommy Smothers, who I listened to on my brother's records. He was pretty funny, and I could do that kind of humor because I really was pretty dense and awkward. To my amazement, it worked, and I actually made Kathy giggle a few times—all at my own expense, of course. Self-deprecation was the way to a woman's heart. It wasn't Bogie and Bergman, but it wasn't Cagney and Jean Arthur, either.

We danced to Skeeter Davis singing about the end of the world and some guy singing about the night. It really didn't matter what songs were playing as long as they were nice and slow and kept playing one after the other without a chance to let go of Kathy. Suddenly the dreams that I had been having were coming true. She was even wearing the red dress that she'd been wearing in my last dream. I had a feeling that I would be having that dream again.

Just as the party was taking off and I was on a roll, Newell's Second Law of Time came into play. This states that minute for minute, good times (and this was turning into a spectacular time) last half as long as school time. Therefore, no sooner had I let go of Kathy's hand than the record came to a stop and Jeannie's mother called down to let us know that it was ten o'clock and time to clean up.

Their parents were picking up Laura and Kathy, so there was no opportunity for Mike and me to walk them home. Apparently, Mike had had the same kind of evening with Laura that I'd had with Kathy. It was all working out as planned.

When we headed home, I left the guys on the corner and walked up Leland Avenue by myself. I was in a daze and just kept thinking about what a great night it had been. I mean, living on Leland Avenue, having the best friends a guy could hope to have, and a family who did everything they could to make me happy, and then having a magical night that I only dared dream about—who could want anything more?

However, I also realized that just as the party zoomed by, so, too, would eighth grade. In all too short a time, we would all be going to different high schools, and I knew it would never be like this again. I knew this was a fleeting time in my life, and I knew Kathy would one day soon walk out of my life just as fast as she had walked into it.

I still can't believe how suddenly she just came out of Laura's house that day and I saw her for the first time as an eighth grader. Well, for the last few months, I couldn't think of anything else but that moment, and now I had spent a whole hour holding her in my arms and uttering a few intelligent sentences. Why worry about a future that hadn't happened yet?

I vowed to enjoy the ride for as long as it lasted so that the rest of eighth grade would be heaven on earth. I would enjoy every single minute, and Kathy would be there beside me. It would be something special.

CHAPTER 4

It Was A Fair Day Indeed.

The rest of that winter was filled with music, and all of it from England. You couldn't turn on a radio without hearing some group from England, yet not one of them could match the Beatles. In fact, for one week, the Beatles had the five top songs of the top ten, and no group or singer had ever done that before. I couldn't imagine it ever being done again.

That is not to say that the other British groups weren't any good. The Rolling Stones, the Searchers, Jerry and the Pacemakers, as well as the Dave Clark Five were all terrific. But the Beatles were always number one. They were so popular that they were even going to make a movie that would be coming out in the summer. It was such a great time in our lives that it was hard to think back to the days of the assassination of President Kennedy.

Before we knew it, March had arrived, and we were entering the last four months of school, the last four months of eighth grade, and our last four months at Blessed Sacrament. The year was going by fast, too fast, and Sister Margaret, along with Father Dolan, and Father Gorman—our parish priests—didn't help things, either. They all went out of their way to make our last few weeks at Blessed Sacrament so special that the time was sure to fly by, and that's the last thing I wanted.

Not that we didn't have schoolwork to do, or homework, for that matter; we had tons. Somehow, though, it all became more interesting than before. Sister Margaret had been teaching us about this dragon lady named Madam Nhu from some country in Asia—South Vietnam I think it was. Anyway, back in the fall we learned that President Kennedy was sending some soldiers to help against the communists who were trying to take over. Now that President

Kennedy was dead, Sister Margaret asked us what we thought the new president, President Johnson, would do.

She also told us some amazing similarities between President Kennedy and President Lincoln. Both were assassinated, which we knew. We also knew that both had vice presidents named Johnson and that each had been elected in the sixtieth year of their respective centuries. She also reminded us that each had defended the rights of the Negroes. What we didn't know was that Lincoln's secretary was named Kennedy and Kennedy's was named Lincoln. This seemed to be a bit too spooky to be a coincidence. Having titillated us (though I'm not sure such a thing can be done by a nun) about these presidential mysteries, she then told us something that would put all of that out of our minds forever and replace it with the miracle of all miracles. We would be taking a class trip! Confused and hesitant to break the spell that had enchanted us, I spoke up, nevertheless, and asked, "What exactly is a class trip?"

The thought of actually leaving the classroom on a school day was too much to ponder—but who could ponder with all the screaming and cheering in Sister Margaret's class at this wondrous news? I mean, the only time we were ever able to leave the classroom during school was when you had to go to confession—not a big treat—or to clap erasers. Sure, you could go to the boys' room once in a while, and I did get to carry the moneybags from Sunday's collection to the bank with the school secretary every Monday, but that was it.

Our typical day started with getting to class, saying the pledge and a morning prayer, schoolwork for three hours, going home for lunch for forty-five minutes, and then another three hours of schoolwork. So a class trip was a really big deal. It didn't even matter to us where we were going until we found out, and then the screaming and cheering really got loud.

The New York World's Fair would be opening in the spring. This was a huge deal as there hadn't been a World's Fair in New York since 1939, which was so long ago it seemed like it was in the last century. It was one of those things that my father always told us about—that, and all the great Yankees games he went to when he was a kid. He saw the Babe, Lou Gehrig, and Jolting Joe, and it is from my father that I inherited my Yankee genes.

The trip to the World's Fair promised to be a great time. We would see Michelangelo's *Pieta*, the famous statue of Mary holding Jesus after he was taken down from the cross, as well as the Goodyear Blimp. Yes, we would see the finest things in art and culture. As Sister Margaret told us all the things that the Fair would have on exposition, it was a shame no one was filming us. Under normal circumstances, we were fifty hormonally explosive teenagers all vying for someone's attention, just trying to get noticed, resorting to any and all obnoxious behaviors to make that happen. Then in a matter of seconds, we were suddenly transformed into a respectful group of well-behaved young adults quietly giving our teacher all the attention she deserved. She never even had to raise her voice once! But as with all good things, our display of civility was short lived.

Sister Margaret concluded her announcement by saying that the buses would pick us up in front of the school and that the trip would take place in two weeks. Mayhem like we had never known followed. It was a good thing we only had a half hour before we were to go home for the weekend. There was no way Sister Margaret could have kept us under control any longer than that.

The raucous behavior continued all the way home. When the guys all found one another on Hoch's Corner, all we could talk about was how we were going to make this class trip a memorable event. We weren't just talking about the *Pieta*, either, let me tell you. No, it wasn't the sights at the fair that we were concentrating on. The focus of our attention was the seats on the bus and who would be sitting in them. A mind may be a terrible thing to waste, but sitting next to the wrong girl on a bus is a fate worse than death. Sitting next to a boy would not do you one bit of good either.

The problem was that we would not all be together on the same bus, so it was going to be hard to orchestrate our seating arrangements without having one another to set screens and picks preventing the wrong person from sitting in the right seat.

Because I was in 8-3, I might very well be by myself while Mike, Freddie, Trent, and PJ would be scattered on other buses. We had to try to work out something, and Mike and Freddie had a plan.

Even with Mike and Freddie working with me, it was still uncertain as to which bus we would get on. There were two eighth-grade buses, and we definitely wanted to be on a bus that Laura and Kathy were on. Freddie had his eye on a girl named Anna, but she was not on the bus we were trying to get on. Like the good friend he was, he helped Mike and me anyway.

The trouble was, Laura and Kathy were getting on a bus with Father Dolan and Father Gorman, and they were with Sister Irene Mary. We had to bite the bullet and try to get on that bus.

When we boarded the bus, it didn't go well at all.

We all jockeyed for position, and Freddie did a great job. He blocked two big guys who were about to jump the line ahead of us. Luckily, we were able to get in and take the last two spots when Sister Irene Mary told the kid behind Freddie to wait for the next bus. I was flying high.

As Mike scooted to the last two seats on the bus, just across from Laura and Kathy, I was attempting to run right behind him. I took a leap and tumbled down the aisle. Hoping my stumble was unnoticed, I was sorely disappointed when Kathy shouted out, "And you said Jimmy couldn't dance!"

Now, ordinarily I would have been humiliated by such a comment, especially since the woman I had the hots for said it. But I wasn't even embarrassed a little bit, as Kathy's comment had the exact opposite effect and gave me a huge boost of confidence and self-esteem.

It seemed that whether it was a huge behemoth of a dog that slapped me to the ground or my own lack of grace, Kathy would continue to acknowledge my existence and call my name. My nothingness had yet again been denied. I got up from the floor and asked Laura to change her seat and sit next to Mike. I then sat next to Kathy and chatted her up as though we were boyfriend and girlfriend. Something had happened that would make the remaining weeks of eighth grade even more special than before.

I no longer talked as though I had marbles in my mouth when I spoke to Kathy. I was witty. I was funny. I was as smooth and debonair as James Bond (or as Mike would say, de-boner). I was making self-deprecating remarks, but all Kathy could do was tell me how funny I was. *My God, what a wonderful world we live in!* I thought with elation. *Here I am about to embark on a journey to explore the wonders of the world, and all I can think about is this thirteen-year-old girl in a Catholic School uniform who thinks I'm funny.*

Freddie was the first to notice my transformation. "Hey, Noodles, what the hell's going on? Did you swallow sex pills or what?"

He looked at Mike and saw that whatever had happened to me had happened to Mike too. Freddie, not wishing to be left behind, looked around and found Diane, who was definitely the prettiest girl in eighth grade, and he persuaded some poor kid to extricate himself from his seat so that he could talk to her. The bus hadn't even started its engine, but we were all revved up.

As you might imagine, the thirty-minute ride from Blessed Sacrament to Flushing, Queens went by in a flash. However, we hit our first obstacle as we made our way off the bus. Even before our feet hit the pavement, Sister Irene Mary called out, "You there, Newell and O'Connor, you will join me over here." Mike and I walked over trying to keep the cursing down to an inaudible growl. Then Kathy did something truly amazing. She lied.

Having seen and heard what was going on, Laura and Kathy put a plan into motion. Kathy approached Sister Irene Mary and said, "Oh, Sister, can we come with you? We just know that seeing the *Pieta* with you will be an enriching, spiritual experience." Mike turned to me and said, "Jimmy, this girl is good; be careful."

The trouble with nuns is that they really fall for that crap if girls offer it. Had O'Connor or I said that, she would have sent us over to Father Dolan for a little spiritual inspiration in the form of a foot. But Kathy? All she had to do was look wide-eyed and innocent with those baby blues and offer that sweet smile, and the good Sister would have given her the keys to the convent, not that anyone would really want them, but you get the point.

Not that I'm complaining, because now all four of us were on our way to explore the world and its fair on a simply gorgeous day in June of 1964, and everything was glorious.

My senses were firing all at once. The sights, sounds, and smells were overpowering, and we hadn't even left the parking lot yet! Just walking next to Kathy was enough to get me going, and as we approached the entrance to the Fair, I couldn't help but laugh.

"Hey, Okie, keep an eye on Noodles; he looks funny."

I turned around to see who had spoken, and Freddie was there shaking his head with a big grin on his face. Next to him were PJ and Trent. Somehow, we were all together and accompanied by a regular bevy of beauts. Now it was time to greet the world of tomorrow.

The first thing we saw as we entered the Fairgrounds was the Unisphere. This was a huge steel globe, surrounded by fountains, which gave us a bird's-eye view of the southern hemisphere. Close by, the tire-shaped Uniroyal Ferris wheel rotated over us. Taking all of it in was so sensational as to inspire vertigo, and I felt myself lose my balance more than once. The guys and I looked around at one another and gave little nods of the head signifying that we knew this was a memory in the making.

Maybe it was the weather, for summer was surely in the air. Maybe it was graduation only being a couple of weeks away. Or maybe, as PJ thought, it was the hormones. Whatever the reason, or whatever the cause, life seemed grand, and our future knew no bounds as it lay before us at the 1964 World's Fair. It was time to leave the Bronx behind, at least for the day.

Technological progress had run amok in the swamps of Flushing Meadow. Futuristic pavilions provided glimpses of a tomorrow that promised peace, tranquility, and unlimited knowledge. And what better way to begin our day than by taking a spin in our own 1964 Ford Mustang? So we headed directly to the Ford pavilion to see what was waiting out there for us.

In addition to getting a history lesson about dinosaurs and cavemen, we also got to see some pretty neat cars of the future. We could have spent an entire day there just sitting behind the wheel of these shiny new vehicles that looked more like small space ships than the cars we had left back on Leland Avenue. The future looked terrific, but the Renaissance attracted our attention next.

The Vatican pavilion was a must for two reasons. First, we were being escorted by a group of nuns led by our principal. That was probably enough of a reason. The second reason, however, made it all worthwhile. For on exposition was Michelangelo's *Pieta*. Now, to be perfectly honest, the Hawaiian pavilion was right next-door, and it probably had hula girls in grass skirts for us to observe and learn from. At the time, this seemed a better option than a hunk of marble situated behind bulletproof glass. But as we made our way to the *Pieta* viewing area one by one, we stopped thinking about the girls next to us and those in the pavilion next door as we took in the eternal beauty that was before us.

Overcome by awe, inspired by the dramatic lighting as stark shadows accented the faces of Jesus and Mary, and reminded of the world we now lived in by the bulletproof glass required to protect this treasure, you could not view the *Pieta* and act like a stupid kid. This singular experience was not wasted on this bunch of TV baby boomers from the Bronx. It was fitting that a relic of a glorious past served as a unique preamble to our journey to the future.

As I came out of the Vatican pavilion, I looked around and realized that the Fair was no mere amusement park with sideshow diversions and a midway full of rides. This was not Freedomland or Steeplechase Park. It was indeed a World's Fair, and the best of twentieth century civilization was on display with no mention of our shortcomings, nor any apology for their omission.

The ability to conquer space, time, and nature offered promise and no retribution. Hope was not bridled by fear. No cloud of pessimism obscured our vision of a better world. Whether it was the IBM, General Electric, or General Motors pavilion, progress knew no bounds. Assassinations, notwithstanding, humankind endures and makes the world a better place.

But enough pontificating; we were off to see some hula girls!

Even though we all knew it was a mistake to let Sister Irene Mary lead us into the Hawaiian pavilion, the hope of seeing scantily clad women was too much to pass up. Our visit didn't last too long. I barely remember seeing something jiggle and shake, and maybe there was a ukulele playing in the background, but before I knew it, I was whisked out the door and on to the next attraction.

The Ice Capades was hardly better, at least in the eyes of the nuns. We were still able to see women in short skating costumes, and every now and then, their male skating partners tossed them up into the air, only to catch them by their crotches. Sister Irene Mary was having a bad interlude.

It got better for her when we went to see the daredevil drivers. Here there would be no sex, just the threat of death and destruction, which was okay in Sister Irene Mary's book. Then it was a quick stop for a Belgian waffle, which ended our daytime activities.

The best part of our day was that, as evening approached, the nuns paid less attention to us than they did to the exhibits. This allowed us to partner up and walk with the girls. As the day transitioned into night, I was reminded once again that the sun was also setting on our grammar school days.

I felt the same way last fall when the Yankees were swept by the Dodgers in the World Series. All good things always come to an end. Mickey Mantle wouldn't always be patrolling center field in Yankee Stadium or smashing home runs in the World Series. Now I realized that I was changing too, and a whole new experience was waiting for me next year. I wasn't thrilled about that, as I had grown comfortable in the eighth grade. I stopped thinking about it as I walked through the Fair, though, and I made an effort to enjoy the wonders around me.

And enjoy I did. There was so much to see that it was hard taking it all in, but then something happened that would completely distract me from the sights and sounds of the World's Fair.

I am not sure if anyone had noticed, and I certainly hoped Sister Irene Mary and Sister Margaret hadn't, but I was overwhelmed by a wave of emotion that sent a shiver up my spine. Not even the Hawaiian hula girls had affected me like this.

Kathy, of course, was the reason for this hormonal spike. There I was lost in thought about high school and change as we were heading toward the gate that we had seemingly just entered a few minutes ago, and Kathy brushed my hand and entwined her pinky in mine. I once got a shock while messing around with my Lionel trains, but that was nothing compared to this. The best part was that I could see the same electricity coursing through her as well. It was as if we were two magnets drawn together.

It only lasted a second or two, but as we parted pinkies, Kathy arched her eyebrows ever so noticeably and smiled a hidden, secretive, but knowing smile. I almost stumbled for the second time that day.

Whatever chance I had of sleeping after such a day was now hopelessly lost to the aftershock of this brief romantic eruption. I would have to make sure to put a new battery in my transistor radio, as this was sure to be a night of fretful tossing and turning, but I would love every agonizing minute of it.

I don't remember much of the bus ride back to school nor of walking home from school afterward. A hot shower (though a cold one probably would have been better), and I was ready for bed if not for sleep. I hooked up the earphone to my radio and tuned in WABC. The tinny voice in my ear proclaimed the start of a British Invasion marathon. The first song was the newest by the Beatles, and it would forever remind me of the events of that terrific day in 1964.

Sometimes people annoy me for reasons that others might think ridiculous, but that is just me being Jimmy. One of the things that always bothered me was the usage of PS when someone was telling me something in conversation. You know, like, "I was talking to this girl, and PS, she was gorgeous." I mean—if it was something you didn't think of including in the beginning, how important was it? It's bad enough when you write that in a letter, but to say it when you are talking? Come on! First of all, do you even know what the bloody PS means? You're saying it to me, and what am I going to do? Am I supposed to read something now? Where does this postscript go when you are talking? Can I say, "Sorry, I won't read to it"? Okay, I'm tired, I had a long, eventful day, and I won't be getting much sleep.

PS—The name of the song that the Beatles were now singing was "P.S. I Love You," and to me at that moment, it was like a Shakespearian sonnet that I would be singing for quite a long time.

I guess I finally did fall asleep, because all of a sudden my mother was waking me up. It was 7:15 a.m., and after my routine ablutions (another *100 Days to Words of Power* word), I sat down to a bowl of Kellogg's Frosted Flakes. I was most off my guard at this time of day, and was even more so today. My mother knew this and would often use this time to her advantage and try to pump me for whatever important and often embarrassing information she might be seeking.

For this reason, it was no surprise to observe her hovering around the stove with nothing on the range or in the oven, though something was definitely cooking. Rather than having to watch her continue this stalking, I finally blurted out, "Why don't you just sit down, and we can get the interrogation over with?"

"And what do you mean by that?" she replied. "It's you who wants to talk to me."

"All right," I said, "let's just say we both want to talk, okay?"

"I'm sure I don't know what you're talking about, but let me begin by asking how your day at the Fair went?"

As I described the previous day's events, I had the impression that she knew more about my day than I did. I told her that we went to see the *Pieta* and then the Ford pavilion. She then interrupted and said, "Don't you mean you went to the Ford pavilion and then to the *Pieta*?"

After realizing what she'd let slip, she shot up from her chair and turned to the stove desperately looking for something to stir or check. Seeing there was nothing to do in the kitchen, she attempted to bolt to the living room, but before she could escape, I intercepted her and shouted, "You knew! How did you know? Mom, I think you have some explaining to do."

It wasn't often that you had the chance to snag your mother, and I would have really enjoyed it had it not been for the fear of what I was about to find out. My mother began her story by stating, "Luv, now I'm still your mother no matter how old you get, and I will always worry about you."

"Ok, Mom, Irish guilt, got it. Can we proceed?"

"Yes, well, your father and I went to the Fair yesterday too, and we happened to see you one or two times."

"You what?"

"Your father and I…"

"I know, one or two times!"

I now felt as though my life was a book that my mother was reading a chapter or two ahead of me. What could I do? I spilled my guts, and all she could say was, "I'm glad you had a good time. Now, off to school, Luv, or you'll be late."

Not wishing to consider what I had just learned, I ran to school with a newfound abandon.

CHAPTER 5

DANCING IN THE DARK.

Graduation was the topic of the day, and it was next to impossible for any of us to contain ourselves. Fortunately, there were those who could contain us, though the good Sisters of Charity would hardly have been enamored by any comparison to containers. Yet, even Sister Margaret, as she spiritually guided us in a law-and-order sort of way, seemed to share our excitement.

Even the other nuns, including Sister Emmaline, had smiles where they usually had scowls. They were almost jolly and had a look of kindness that we had never seen before. Mind you, I still wouldn't risk the wrath of their anger by exhibiting a scintilla of deviant behavior. But it was still a relief to see them smile.

Of course, we still had schoolwork and finals to worry about. All our exams would be Diocesan tests and could not be taken lightly. Yet, they didn't scare us as they once did. So, after a few hours of work, the rest of the day consisted of graduation practice, group discussions on current events, and general socializing. We even persuaded Sister Margaret to allow us to listen to records.

Although Sister Margaret was nice, dancing, especially slow dancing, was not allowed; she hadn't totally lost her mind. However, I may have.

I remember one of our teachers saying, "Music hath charms that soothe the savage beast" (breast being a term not used in Catholic school unless you were referring to an order of chicken). Well, whoever authored that phrase evidently had not heard the Beatles sing "Twist and Shout."

Sister Margaret had only stepped out for a second. It was at that precise moment that John Lennon began wailing and for some reason, I thought it would be a good idea to stand on Sister Margaret's desk and sing along. This led to utter chaos of the type not seen in Blessed Sacrament during my eight years there. Everyone was singing, and we got quite loud. So loud, in fact, that our voices carried down to the principal's office and interrupted Sister Irene Mary's phone call to some head nun. This was not good.

Sister Margaret was a good sport and had a smile on her face, but that didn't last long. I guess she could see what we were in for through the window of the door, as her face seemed to grow an eerie shade of green. By the time I noticed this, the door to our classroom flew open and a bellowing voice interrupted the Beatles and the rest of us. "What do you think you are doing on top of that desk, Mr. Newell?" (I never liked the sound of Mr. Newell; it's right up there with James Peter Newell.)

I hadn't the nerve to turn around and look at the face I knew to be Sister Irene Mary's. I just got down off the desk and looked for a place to hide. "Turn around and face me!" I started to do another impersonation. It was not John Lennon this time nor any of the Beatles. As I turned to face my peril, I went into my best Ralph Kramden voice, saying, "Homina, Homina, Homina."

I think Sister Irene Mary thought I had started to sing in Latin this time. This helped a little, actually. I was then instructed to join her in her office. I turned around to look at my classmates and Sister Margaret one last time. I walked toward the door like Jimmy Cagney going to the chair in *Angels with Dirty Faces*. When I got to the office, I was instructed to sit in the chair. I looked for a plug. There was no plug, but that did not mean I wouldn't suffer.

As I sat there staring at all the things in the principal's office, I could only think of all my efforts for so many years to avoid this very fate. I had seen kids come and go in grammar school, all willing to take chances and face the principal's office, only never to be seen again.

Banishment to public school had been their fate. All I could think about was what would be mine. All the pictures of Jesus and Mary only reinforced the thought that I was in it deep. Getting snagged the week before graduation is kind of funny when you think about it, though. I could see my parents having a big laugh when I told them. Well, that was a thought anyway.

I must have sat there an hour or so, but when I looked up at the clock, it read 2:45 p.m. I had only been there fifteen minutes! This must be some *Twilight Zone* thing again. Watching the second hand creep around the face of that clock was as much torture as I could endure. Finally, it was 3:45 p.m. The door opened and out came a woman who was best friends with Kathy's mother. It just kept getting better.

She didn't make eye contact, which made it worse. Well, if my parents were going to kill me, I guess it didn't matter if Kathy dumped me. The good news was I stopped watching the clock. I couldn't read it anyway through the tears.

I had almost started to nod off when I heard the floor creak in Sister Irene Mary's office. I tried desperately not to think evil thoughts as to why the floor was creaking; I did not want to be laughing when she opened the door. When I looked up at the clock and saw that it was 5:00 p.m., she came out and asked me how I was doing!

I didn't respond because I didn't know what to say. Then she said, "Considering how loud you play your music, I can only assume that you have experienced hearing loss, so I say again; how are you doing out here?"

A little shocked by the pleasantness in her voice, I stammered, "Very well, thank you, Sister."

She then said, "James, I trust you will confine yourself to your desk, preferably sitting in it rather than hoofing on it, and that the only songs emanating from your golden throat will be those Latin hymns comprising our graduation ceremony. Do you think you can comply with these rather innocuous restrictions?"

"Oh, sure, Sister."

"Then you may go," she responded.

"Thank you, Sister."

That was it? No call home? No ruler over the knuckles? No banishment from graduation? Oh, baby!

The sigh of relief that I exhaled almost made me dizzy.

When I got out of the office, everyone was waiting for me. Some looked pretty disappointed when I came out with the news that I'd been let off easy. Apparently, a pool had been organized regarding the outcome of my afternoon's misadventure. Unfortunately for all the participants, scot-free was not on the table, so all bets were off. Now we were on to more important matters, as the first graduation party was scheduled for tonight, and we had to go home and get ready.

Naturally, Laura and Kathy would be there. In fact, had it not been for them, we wouldn't have been invited. The kid having the party was a friend of theirs, and they put the squeeze on him and got us all invited. He needed girls to attend his party, and we were the price he had to pay to get them, at least two of them. So Mike, Freddie, Trent, and PJ were all going to be there with me hoping for good things to happen.

There was no time to make plans, as we all had to go home, have dinner, and shower. The latter activity caused a little consternation for my parents as I literally jumped into the shower as soon as I got in the door. I could hear my father proclaiming loudly, "Have you ever seen him move so quickly into the shower? Jesus, Mary, and Joseph, if he could move that fast all the time, he could play center field for the Yankees."

Having showered, I looked to see if I needed a shave, forgetting for the moment that I was not Trent. I bolted to my bedroom where my brother Michael was listening to records and then watched, as I got dressed. He just had to make a few suggestions. "First, you need something for that hair and, no offense, you need this." He took a bottle of Old Spice and applied a rather abundant amount to my neck and cheeks. It burned like a sonova...sorry.

Then he doled out a little dab of Brylcreem to my hair so that I was now lubed up and ready to go. Having been so dolled up for the evening's festivities, but, I guess, sporting a little too much in the Old Spice department, my parents did not subject me to the usual third degree and actually looked relieved to see me leave. I was halfway down Leland Avenue before I realized that I had not eaten dinner. It was not like me to miss a meal, but tonight I had no appetite. Even so, when I got to Hoch's I picked up a pack of Yankee Doodles and washed it down with a five-cent Coke.

In the midst of my repast, I was joined by my brethren who were equally decked out in their finest threads and emitting an olfactory smorgasbord of colognes and/or deodorants. It was a big night. They, too, had forsaken home-cooked meals in lieu of Hoch's finest baked goods and quaffs. Maybe all this sugar would make us better dancers?

We were a group of considerable mention consisting of Mike, Trent, PJ, Freddie, George, Eddy, and yours truly. We made our way down Gleason Avenue heading toward St. Lawrence where our host, Albert, lived. Along the way, we were intercepted by the girls, who were waiting at the corner of Thieriot. Laura and Kathy were there—thank Heaven—as well as Roe, Jeannie, Theresa, and Anne. I hoped another girl was coming, or else one of us would go home disappointed, not to mention poor Albert.

Mike and I gravitated toward the rear of the group, as did Laura and Kathy—so far so good. The girls were in between Mike and me. We were like two lucky pieces of bread comprising a delicious sandwich. As if we had choreographed our movements, Mike and I each made a rather subtle yet highly successful move to brush the hand of our partner. Reminiscent of my experience at the World's Fair, the resulting chemical reaction when our hands met was nothing short of atomic.

Throwing caution to the wind, I looked at Mike, he at me, we gave each other the Go sign, and we were off. We both simultaneously took the plunge and made a hurried grasp for our true love's hand.

I was met by a warm yet very willing hand that made sure I would not-could not let go. It was exhilarating. Just as I had grasped Kathy's hand, we saw Father Dolan walking out of the Rectory gate toward the corner of Taylor Avenue. When they saw him, Laura and Kathy made a beeline and ran to him leaving Mike and me in a state of confusion. We were stunned. How could they be running there when we were holding their hands here?

Our befuddlement was soon replaced by sheer and utter horror as we looked at each other realizing that the hands that had been so warm and willing were each other's. We quickly shook our hands off and looked around in relief. No one had seen our mistaken handholding. No one ever found out, especially Laura and Kathy.

Mike and I would not have survived such a scandal. We never could have been seen alone together ever afterward or even standing next to each other in a football huddle. The thought of hiking the ball to each other was out of the question regardless of the fact that no one knew.

Mike and I quickly put this incident behind us and made off to greet Father Dolan to whisk the girls to Albert's and to our first graduation party.

When we got to Albert's house, he had a stack of 45s on the record player all ready to go that would ensure at least a half hour of non-stop dancing. Each record was slower than the one before. I began chanting, "Hormones to the left of me, hormones to the right of me volleyed and thundered." Freddie shouted out that I was on sex pills again. Then all of a sudden, Mike and I were in a side room and were joined by Laura and Kathy. Someone put the lights out as Jerry and the Pacemakers were heard singing, "Don't Let the sun catch you crying."

Fearing that we might be caught, and not wishing to get Albert in trouble, I searched for the light switch. As I groped the wall, each of my three companions asked in a shouted whisper what I was doing. When I told them I was looking for the light, their responses were both swift and decisive as I was subjected to pokes, kicks, and a slap to the back of my head. Mike took hold of me and said, "Think, Jimmy, think!" But I was too dazed from being throttled to think.

Laura then said, "What's the matter, Jimmy? Don't you want to dance with Kathy?" I couldn't think of anything to say.

By this time, Kathy could see that I wasn't getting it, so she finally put her arm around me and started dancing with me again, this time closer than I thought humanly possible. "I think what we're trying to say is that maybe we should conserve energy and not waste electricity," she said. And so, in our effort to promote lower electric bills, we danced in the dark, and to conserve our own energy, we only moved very slowly.

After four or five records, it got awfully quiet. About five minutes went by, and I realized there was no music being played. We could hear people in the next room yelling at Albert to put more records on. It was then that he came into our room and found the light switch that had eluded me a half hour earlier. He was looking for records, but when he put the lights on, he looked as though he had just caught his wife in a compromising position. I remember Ricky having that look in an *I Love Lucy* episode.

I'm not sure what hurt more, the lights flashing in my eyes or having to let go of Kathy.

Albert was about to have a tizzy when Laura and Kathy, like soldiers jumping on a live grenade to save their comrades, made the ultimate sacrifice; each begged him to dance with her next. The unsuccessful supplicant, Laura, came back to Mike smiling at her good fortune (and ours). Kathy, on the other hand, had to dance with Albert.

The party was in full swing, and it was only 9:05 p.m. Although we didn't get to repeat our earlier escapade, at least Kathy didn't have to dance with

Albert anymore. She did, however, dance with me one more time. Fortunately, it was a pretty long dance that lasted from 9:05 p.m. until we heard "Goodnight Sweetheart" at eleven o'clock.

This was only the first of many graduation parties, but as far as I was concerned, none was better than Albert's. Although I knew I would get a lot more opportunities to dance with Kathy, I had the feeling that I would never again dance with her the way I did that night.

But it was still tonight for a bit longer, and tomorrow had to wait.

Hoping to keep the magic of this night going, Mike and I attempted to persuade the girls to take the long way home. Amazingly, they agreed, and now we had to invent the long way home.

I don't know why I felt this was a once in a lifetime moment that would never be repeated, but I guess this thought affected me. I grew quiet, and Mike must have sensed this because he tried to joke me out of my mood. "Hey, Stanley, what are you looking for, a light to switch on?" That was all I needed; the girls laughed, so I was forced out of my coma and back to the magic of the moment.

Kathy sensed what I was thinking and held my hand as we walked down Gleason Avenue. All was right with the world. Despite all our efforts to make this a really long walk, we arrived at Kathy's house too soon. Now we had to say goodnight, but how? It seemed like neither one of us knew what to do next, or maybe we were afraid of what we knew.

Then all of a sudden, we each made up our minds. Kathy bobbed and I weaved, so neither one of us could land a glove or a kiss on the other. The moment our lips made contact, a light in the backyard came on. This signaled the end of the night. Kathy turned and walked up the long driveway where an eternity ago her dog had flattened me.

I thought of how I used to look up that driveway hoping to catch a glimpse of her but never succeeding, but I had never felt as sad then as I did now.

I stood at the bottom of that driveway desolate, and then it got worse. The light in the backyard went out, and with it went any glimmer of hope of completing the kiss. As I turned from the driveway, I was jolted by something indefinable, and I feared for my safety.

Still feeling the aftereffects from the pokes and prods of when I stupidly looked for the light switch, I braced myself for another thrashing. But what struck me was something I was totally unprepared for.

I was smacked right in the mouth by the two sweetest lips in the universe. She must have kissed me for twenty seconds, and then Kathy said, "I couldn't let you go without saying goodbye, and without letting you know I had the best time ever, and that I'll always remember this night."

Well, you could have run me over with a '58 Mercury! I was numb. I was hoping to never wake up from this dream. I wanted this feeling to never leave me. But after a few minutes I was back from my reverie and Kathy was gone. I looked around and Mike and Laura were coming toward me. Laura looked shocked, and Mike was smirking and busting to say something, but Laura directed him back down Leland Avenue.

It was clear that Mike and I had some talking to do before we each went home. So, as he was being led by Laura toward her house, he called out for me to meet him on Hoch's Corner to reconnoiter, as he liked to say.

While I waited for Mike, Freddie, Trent, and PJ all came to the corner, each having walked their respective dates for the evening back home. We all had the same sheepish grin indicating that we'd all had a successful night. Despite the desire to maintain our reputations for kissing without telling (well, now that we all had actually kissed someone, we had a reputation to maintain), telling was exactly what we wanted to do. Then our silence was interrupted.

Mike could be heard singing as he jitterbugged like Fred Astaire around the corner of Thieriot and headed up Gleason Avenue. When he saw us huddled outside Hoch's, he started yelling my name. "Jim-m-a-a-ay!"

I asked, "So, did you break my record for kissing?"

"Hey, buddy boy," he replied. "First of all, I didn't think I could hold my breath that long, but before I could find out, Fulda opened the door and caught us mid-kiss."

"Who the heck is Fulda?" we all asked at once.

"Oh, that's Laura's mother," Mike answered.

"So, we're on a first-name basis with the mother-in-law?" PJ asked.

"Does she call you Okie?" Trent wanted to know.

"Hey, forget that," Mike began. "You should have seen our Mr. Newell in action. I thought he was going to pass out after Kathy got through with him."

"I told you he was still taking those sex pills, and this time he OD'd," Freddie chimed in.

PJ then said, "Come on, guys, we all need a good, cold shower, and this is a school night; believe me, you all need your beauty rest."

As the others went on their way, Mike and I dawdled just a bit to recap our pre-summer adventure.

"You know, this is a night I'll remember for a long time."

"I know—it almost seems like a dream that I am going to wake up from," I agreed.

"Yeah, you looked like you were in a daze when we left the party, and I got the feeling you were getting all sad and all," Mike said.

"I wasn't really depressed or anything, but I felt kind of weird. I just felt like something really cool was coming to an end, but not just the party, and I was wondering what would come next. It was like during graduation practice. It felt great that we were almost out of grammar school, but I got nervous thinking about next year and high school."

"Hey, listen, after that marathon smooch, you can skip high school and go right to college, Jimmy Boy."

"You know what I mean. Besides, it really wasn't that long of a kiss."

"Wasn't that long? By the time you two finished I needed to shave again!"

"Oh, well, I guess we better head home. We do have school tomorrow and another party tomorrow night."

"Hey, Jimbo, don't be getting too much sleep; you're too beautiful as it is."

"I know you mean well, Mike. But, hearing that from the man with whom I so recently held hands is not the thought I want to leave with."

"Damn, why did you have to remind me about that? Now I won't be able to sleep."

Laughing as I headed up Leland, I said, "Goodnight, Mike, see you tomorrow."

Mike turned and began singing "Goodnight Sweetheart" in his best doo-wop voice.

I turned around and shouted back at him, "You better be singing that to Laura and not to me." With that, we both went home.

I guess I had a good night's sleep because no sooner had my head hit the pillow than my alarm clock was ringing. Miraculously, I showered, got dressed, and even gulped down a little breakfast with nary a word from my mother. To be honest, I expected an updated version of the Inquisition, but maybe because I had three more parties to go, she just couldn't be bothered pumping me for details from the night before. I was not complaining. I was just as happy to scoot off to Blessed Sacrament for the last time.

CHAPTER 6

Is Commencement The End?

I had entered Blessed Sacrament in September of 1956. I can still remember climbing the four stories to the top floor of the old school building crying my eyes out on my first day. My first grade teacher, Mrs. Gallo, was so nice, and I eventually settled down, but I can still remember how I felt that first day. It was that day that I met Mike. He sat right alongside of me, so I guess the day wasn't all that bad.

Now, eight years later, I am going to school once more with tears in my eyes.

It was still pretty early, so I went to Hoch's and read the sports page of the *Daily News*.

Yogi Berra had replaced Ralph Houk as theYankee manager, and he seemed to be as good a manager as he had been a catcher. I left the store to head to school after having read all that I wanted to read, and saving a nickel to boot. I looked down Leland in the hope that Kathy might be coming, and to my astonishment and great joy, she was.

I guess I didn't believe my eyes because, out of habit, I turned around to walk down Gleason toward school. After I realized that I had in fact seen Kathy coming, I stopped dead in my tracks and reversed direction. She laughed and shook her head as she approached, and I needn't bother to ask what was so funny. It was enough that she was happy.

I was amazed. After months of trying to time my schedule just right in the hopes of meeting Kathy on the way to school, here I was on the very last day getting it just right.

We walked together down Gleason, and as we made it to the corner of Thieriot, Mike and Laura met us. We all had the same gleam in our eyes, consisting of equal parts of sheer joy and sadness caused by coming-of-age. All of a sudden, I thought about Peter Pan.

I nodded at Mike, and he said, "C'mon, let's go to school."

Maybe it was due to my love of history, or maybe I'm just a sentimental fool, but instead of going to our usual spot in the schoolyard, I took a brief detour toward the old school. I looked up to the fourth floor and the spires of the church. I understood how a six-year-old could be so overwhelmed after entering its doors. More than ever, it reminded me of a castle, but now as I approached my fourteenth birthday and was about to graduate, I was more afraid of leaving than I had been when I first went in.

On impulse, I ran into the building, made my way up to the fourth floor, and headed to my first-grade classroom. I just wanted to look in, and I didn't think anyone would be there to see me. However, as I gazed into the room, I saw Mrs. Gallo helping a little kid get ready for the day. She looked up and saw me looking in. She came over to me and said, "Good morning, James. Ready for the big day?" I nodded yes, and she then reminded me to come back later with my autograph book.

I went back to the schoolyard and met up with the gang. It was still pretty early, so we had some time to spend before going to class. I looked around at my friends: Mike, PJ, Trent, Freddie, Laura, and Kathy. I wondered where we were all headed.

We all started talking, and thoughts of the future were limited to tonight's party and tomorrow's graduation ceremony. I guess we all had mixed emotions about things, as our normal verbal jousting was replaced by the unspoken realization that this was it. This would be the last time we would meet here at this place.

I think the guys knew that we were friends for life and that, no matter where the future would bring each of us; the connection among us would always remain.

We might all be going to different high schools, but we would continue to be together in the best neighborhood money could buy. In keeping with the solemnity of the moment, we readied ourselves for the all-important ritual of the signing of the autograph books.

We had been given our books the day before, but today we would share all of our good wishes with one another. Nevertheless, the temptation to write something obscene was quite real, especially if you were handed a book while in a crowd and could dispose of it quickly without it being noticed that you had signed it.

If you really wanted to be nasty, you could sign one page with "Good luck in high school" or something like that, and then slip in another page with a more risqué entry, maybe signing someone else's name. As we started this routine, Laura and Kathy ran over to some of their girlfriends.

We guys all started to recite things that we would have loved to put in different people's books, and most of these were beyond risqué, when all of a sudden Father Gorman broke into our conversation. Now, we weren't sure just how much he had heard, so we dumbed it up and acted real casual and innocent.

"You know, I was just saying to Father Dolan and Monsignor Hart that we would miss this graduating class, especially the boys. They are all such fine examples of good, young, Catholic men in both behavior and speech. Wouldn't you agree, Jimmy?"

Ok, he was letting me know I was snagged.

"Absolutely, Father. In fact, Michael here was saying the exact same thing not a minute ago."

"Is that so? That must have been when he was comparing you to a certain Catholic from Calcutta."

No one came to my rescue, and they all looked around for an opportunity to escape. We were caught in the act, and it was each man for himself.

Looking for a way out, I finally said, "Hey, Father, I wanted to thank you again for the five bucks for getting a hundred on the Nutty Ned Test." He had given us this test at the end of April, and we had to identify things that he had taught us during the year. It was more of a "What's wrong with this picture?" kind of thing, and I had been the only one in the eighth grade to ace it. I wanted to remind him that he was supposed to give me ten bucks as a prize, and that giving another kid half my winnings because she came close was bullshit, but I used some judgment here.

"That's quite okay, Jimmy, you were the only one to get a hundred, so you deserved it."

"Oh, I know, Father. In fact, I remember that no one had ever gotten a hundred before."

"Yes, James, that is true, and I am glad that you are so attentive to what I say." With that, he smiled and shook his head, and then he headed to the rectory.

Now you would have thought that, having flirted with disaster, we would have learned our lesson and given up our quest for poetic dominance. Not so. We just learned to be more circumspect in our recitations and made damn sure no adult was in earshot of our verbal expositions. Having exhausted our repertoire, we were now ready to face the day.

A few minutes later, Sister Irene Mary came out of the back door of the convent, and we all knew what was coming. We all got butterflies as we prepared ourselves for the last bell. The first bell rang, and then finally, the last bell. We looked around, nodded to one another, and made our way to the second floor of the new school for the last time.

Any ambivalence I may have been experiencing was soon swept away as I entered my classroom. You just couldn't be melancholy on the last day of school. We took our seats, and shortly thereafter, we rose for morning prayer and saluted the flag. After one hour of graduation practice, we were free to roam the school unattended for our autograph hunt.

So, I set off with Mike to the old school with our autograph books in hand. I guess getting some of our old teachers to sign them would be a nice thing. It might even make us look sensitive to Kathy and Laura. Our first stop was Miss Hannigan's class. She was Mike's fourth grade teacher, and she had taught everyone in my family except me. I guess that entitled me to have her sign my book even though she hadn't been one of my teachers.

We filed in together, and as I waited for Mike to schmooze with Miss H, I stood around biding my time. Soon I noticed one of the kids in the class looking up at me from her desk. She was a little redhead who looked vaguely familiar. Seeing her staring at me, I said, "So, what's your story?"

"Do you want me to sign your book?" she asked.

I said, "Sure, why not."

She took my book and kind of huffed as she did so. I asked her what the problem was. She said, "You could have been more excited than 'Sure why not' that's all you could say?"

At that moment, I noticed that she had the biggest and bluest eyes I had ever seen, and there was more than a hint of fire in them. I couldn't believe that this little pipsqueak of a fourth grader was giving me a hard time about how I wasn't "excited" about her signing my book.

"I'm sorry," I said. "Would you please sign my autograph book? I would really like it if you did." Well, those were magic words, and the fire in those big blues was replaced by…let's just say she made me very uncomfortable. She was only a fourth-grader after all!

Well, one of her friends was close by, and she asked, "Now that wasn't so hard, was it? That was the way you should have spoken to her in the first place."

I said, "Who are you, her lawyer?"

She said, "My name is Sonia, and I'll sign that for you too."

Not wishing to set her off, I said, "Thank you; please do."

I was reading what the two of them wrote, and as I left, I said to the little redhead, "See you around, Eileen."

She replied, "You will in about seven years." I shook my head not knowing what the heck she meant by that, but I had a strange feeling that I would find out.

I then split up with Mike and headed to Mrs. Gallo's class and then Mrs. Cappazola's, who still called me John even though she had taught my brother Johnny seventeen years before she had me. She actually wrote Dear John in my book and got really embarrassed about it, but I told her not to worry because even my father called me Johnny. Next came Miss Mangan, and then Mrs. Riley before I headed back to the new school. It had been built in 1955, but I guess it would forever be known as the new school.

As I headed down the stairs, I ran into Al, the custodian. I asked him if he would sign my book. He was busy mopping up the floor. At first, I thought he might be annoyed to have to stop, but he took the book and smiled as he signed it. He gave it back to me and said, "Thanks. Thanks a lot."

Back at the new school, I got all my teachers' signatures. That didn't take too long, and then I went after my fellow graduates making sure that some wise ass did not victimize me. When all was said and done, none of us did anything too reprehensible, as we all knew our parents would be reading our books, but it was fun just thinking about what you would like to write.

Mike, Laura, Kathy, and I wrote in one another's books, and we all wrote silly poems, but I was sure that when I would read them forty years later, they would make me feel as good as they did then.

The time for dismissal was rapidly approaching. Always a time of heightened anticipation, the last hour of this particular school year was especially poignant. It was our last hour at Blessed Sacrament, and all the things that went on in our last year seemed to flash before my eyes.

The Kennedy assassination, the Beatles, and the World's Fair were enough to make this a memorable year, but my friends were what made it special. They at least would not be left behind with the memories.

The last few minutes went by as my classmates talked and reminisced. I remained quiet, lost in my thoughts. Then George came in with a camera. It was one of the new Kodak Instamatic cameras that had a flashcube instead of individual flash bulbs. This was pretty neat, as you could take four pictures without changing the bulb.

I grabbed George and we both headed to 8A 1 to get Laura and Kathy and then next door to 8A 2 to get Mike. I got George to take four pictures of us as a group so that we could each have one. Just as the last dot flashed before our eyes, the crackle of the intercom announced that the dismissal bell was about to be rung.

We disassembled and headed to our classrooms to say the Angelus one last time, and then goodbye to eighth grade.

At the end of the prayer, Sister Margaret started to speak but then stopped abruptly. Some of us wanted to say something, too, but somehow the words never came out. I guess our goodbyes had to wait until tomorrow after graduation. The bell rang and summer vacation began. You couldn't hear a pin drop. You couldn't hear anything but kids screaming.

No matter how sad it was to leave Blessed Sacrament, the last day of school was just about the most amazing thing you could ever imagine. I can't believe that there will ever be anything as good as the last day of school. Even a long, drawn-out, hot graduation ceremony could not dampen our sense of freedom. School was out and the living was easy.

As I started the walk home on Taylor Avenue, I met up with Mike on the corner of Gleason. We decided to wait for Laura and Kathy. They always took a little longer; why that was we could never figure out. They finally appeared and looked as though they were happy that we had waited. We made plans for the party that night, which would be at Ro's.

Mike suggested that we give the girls our blue ties as a gift of some sort to commemorate our last day at BSS. The girls took our ties without comment, which was probably a good thing. Before we parted company with them, we agreed that we would pick them up at Laura's house at seven.

As soon as we were alone, Mike and I started talking about the lameness of what had just happened. We vowed to make amends, but how? "Flowers, my boy," said Mike. "We have to get them flowers for the party—a corsage, you know?"

"Yeah, you're right there, Mr. O. We must get them flowers."

We agreed to meet at six and to head over to the Circle Florist where we could get a nice corsage. Since we knew the owners, we let them think that the flowers were for our mothers. No sense exposing us to the usual ribbing that such a purchase might bring. As we made our way back to Hoch's corner, each with box in hand, we anticipated how the girls would react to our five dollar and twenty-five cent purchases.

What we didn't anticipate were the fateful words, "Oh, how beautiful. Please put it on me."

I should point out that these were not wrist corsages with an elastic band that stretched over the waiting hand. No, these corsages had to be pinned onto their chests! I looked at Mike, and the devilish grin that had suddenly appeared on his face had as quickly given way to a countenance struck with fear.

"Well, Stanley, here's another fine mess you've gotten me into," I said as I shook my head at him.

The irony of our situation made matters worse. What had been the subject of countless hours of teenage lust was staring us right in the face, and we cowered at the sight. Our hands were dripping wet. Our ties got unbearably tight.

I started to take the pin out of the corsage and dropped it. I dropped it again and a third time. Finally Laura said, "Gimme that. I'll do it. Kathy, you'll have to do mine, Mike looks like he will pass out."

From that point on, Laura and Kathy felt assured that their virtue would remain intact.

Regardless of our floral misadventure, we got to Ro's and had another great time. Though we did not repeat our dance in the dark, we danced enough with Laura, Kathy, and the other girls in our group, and we all had a grand time. The night ended early as we all had a busy day the next day. Even the guys headed home early.

Saturday morning of June 20, 1964 was warm and humid, and promised to be even warmer and more humid as the day wore on—perfect cap and gown weather. I wanted to start a pool on the number of people who would pass out in church. It would be packed, as over one hundred and fifty kids were graduating, and you could figure that each kid would have three or four sweltering guests cramming the pews.

As usual, we could expect the old man who spent all his waking hours in the church praying and hacking up a lung and expectorating in a brown paper bag. That was always a nice touch on a hot day. We often wondered what he had done as a young man that demanded such a degree of repentance.

Graduation would include a High Mass that we would sing in Latin, also a treat on a hot day.

I had a glass of orange juice for breakfast, took a shower, and made my way to school with cap and gown in hand. It was nine o'clock; a full hour before the Mass, and already the schoolyard was jammed with graduates. We mingled and said our goodbyes knowing that for some, we would never see one another again.

It was interesting to see the reaction that everyone had to the day. While some were the same as they always were, which was not that nice, others really appreciated the magnitude of the day. One of the girls, who was number one on everyone's list as the sexiest girl in school, came up to me, planted a big kiss on me, and told me I was one of the nicest guys she had ever known. Another girl said the same thing, but she didn't attack me. I was liking it so far.

Father Dolan and Father Gorman came around to wish us good luck and had nothing but nice things to say. You could tell they were really proud of us and that they would miss us. The nuns came out and made us feel the same way. Then it was time to line up for graduation.

By now our families, friends, and casual passersby without a real life of their own were filing into the pews of the church. Mrs. Molito, the organist, was sitting in front of her organ in the choir loft, fingers at the ready. If my calculations were correct, it would be one hundred and seventeen degrees inside.

Sure enough, as we entered the church, the heat hit us like a brick wall. Then the bellowing of Mrs. Molito's organ blasted us with "Pomp and Circumstance," and I could just hear my father say, "Give her a towel," as my mother, along with every other mother in the church, was already crying.

The graduates were lined up, supposedly in size places with girls forming one line, boys the other. As luck would have it, Kathy was one girl behind my partner who happened to be the homeliest girl in creation. Well, I couldn't take this, and I had to do something, so when the nuns were looking elsewhere, I bent down to tie my shoe.

Despite wearing my brother Michael's new loafers, this worked like a charm, and I pushed the kid behind me up one place and I took his, right next to Kathy. By the time he realized what I had done, it was too late and he was stuck with his new, homely partner.

Kathy and I walked down the aisle of Blessed Sacrament and then quickly separated and entered our respective pews. The ceremony and Mass seemed to fly by, mercifully. We received our diplomas, moved our tassels from one side of our caps to the other, and all of a sudden, we were graduates of elementary school.

We all hung around outside for a little while, just enough to say some more goodbyes and then meet up with our families. Then, we all separated and made our way to our family celebrations. My Aunt Catherine and Uncle Al as well as Uncle James and Aunt Celia were there along with all my brothers, my sister Barbara, and their kids. My brother Michael stared at his new loafers and admired how they looked. Margaret, his girlfriend, was also with him. She liked them too and told Michael he should get a pair. He said he already had a pair exactly like them. I sheepishly looked for somebody else to talk to.

We all made our way home to 1261 Leland, and my father immediately got the fans going as it was nearly as hot in our apartment as it had been in church. We had been there for about a half hour when my father asked me in his loud voice, "Did you say hello to Aunt Catherine?"

Now, Aunt Catherine was my godmother, and she was the first one I had greeted at the church nearly two hours ago. I said hello again and gave her a nice kiss, and I thanked her for the graduation gift and the money she had given me when the graduation ceremony was over, but somehow my father thought I might have forgotten to say hello to Aunt Catherine. The unfortunate thing is that he would ask me the same question yet again in an hour or so.

The only people who were not there were my sister Maureen and brother-in-law Hank and their kids. Maureen had just had my latest niece, Marybeth, eight days ago, so I was told she had not been able to make the trip up from Atlantic Highlands. But no sooner had I thought about her than Michael announced that they had just pulled up in their van. I guess Maureen really needed to get out of the house. I wasn't sure exactly what went on in childbirth (or at conception, either), but I imagined it was something that you didn't want to hop in a car and travel for two hours right after.

Anyway, now my relatives would be occupied by the new baby, and I would no longer be subjected to the cheek squeezes and wet kisses laced with Ballantine beer. Fortunately, I still got the cards laced with cash.

After lunch we watched a Yankees game, had some cake, and before we knew it, the day was over and everyone was preparing to leave. I helped my mother and father clean up, and then I made an early retreat to the back bedroom with my transistor radio and went to bed.

As I thought about being a grammar school graduate, I considered how both my parents had not gone to school beyond the eighth grade. They might be considered uneducated by some people. The truth was, however, they were smarter and more sophisticated in the ways of the world that really mattered than many people who were considered educated.

My mother wasn't just a great cook and homemaker. She was as much an educator as any teacher I ever had. Her sense of humor, her sayings, and her

Shakespearian quotes came from a lifetime of reading that belied her lack of a formal education. Her own mother, Mary Dowd, was the source of much of her wisdom. My mother always used sayings that she had heard her mother say, and while some drove me crazy, such as, "Don't let little things bother you," they almost always contained nuggets of wisdom. Her greatest gift was that she imparted this love of knowledge to her children- most of them anyway.

My mother would often say to me, "You're a pain in the Gazandy Bag." I was unsure of why I was, nor could I tell you what or where my mother's Gazandy Bag was, but rest assured, I did cause her discomfort, nonetheless.

I started thinking about the time she had to go to the school doctor with me. I remember he caused me a certain amount of pain and quite a bit of discomfort. I must have been in the first grade, and the doctor was so fat he could barely sit in the same room while behind his desk as he talked to my mother. "Mrs. Newell, James will have to watch his weight."

To which I replied to my mother, "Ma, this fat bastard is telling *me* to lose weight?" Actually, I only thought that, as I would never talk like that to my mother out of fear of distressing her Gazandy Bag.

I should note that I am not sure of the proper spelling of Gazandy Bag, and I couldn't say if it should be capitalized, but I have utilized creative license here, just so you know. Come to think of it, my mother did have an operation when I was five, and I never knew what it was for. Maybe she had a Gazandy Bagectemy? No, that couldn't be it, as I continued to be a pain in her Gazandy Bag for many years hence.

After the fat-ass doctor told my mother that I had to lose weight, he went on to take the family history. "So, Mrs. Newell, I see you have five children."

"Yes, and I lost two," she replied.

"Holy shit!" I screamed. Well, of course, I didn't really, but I made damn sure she never let go of my hand on our walk home.

—ᨓ—

My father, on the other hand, was bestowed with a more pragmatic approach to education and other of life's necessities. His degree was awarded by the School of Hard Knocks. Having to leave school while still a child so that he could get a job to help his family, Michael A. Newell was truly a man of the twentieth century. He worked hard and learned much from working. There was little that he did not know about things mechanical.

Despite a propensity for breaking glassware (I'd always hear him say, "I swear it walked off the counter"), I could always rely on him to fix my bike or my locomotive. Perhaps the coolest thing he did was to affix a steering wheel from a Buick onto my bike in lieu of handlebars.

My father was a baseball player, and in his day, he had played catcher for the Con Edison team. He wore his broken fingers as a merit badge. Despite the fact that by the time I came around he resembled Saint Anthony in the hair department, pictures of him when he was young depicted a twentieth century man on the make, a real stud.

I never understood why my father's friends called him the Tasheroo Kid, but they must have had a pretty good reason, and he seemed to wear this as a merit badge, too.

Although he always lived in an apartment, he had the skills to build a house. His real education came during the Great Depression. It was during that time when he learned that work of any type was a noble experience. He got a job with Con Edison in 1930 when jobs were hard to come by. After working there for several months, and with the effects of the Depression worsening for the company, he was told that he was going to be laid off. When he heard this, he immediately went to see one of the vice presidents and made his pitch to be kept on.

He let the vice president know that my mother was going to have a baby and that he would do any job assigned. My father's determination and willingness to work hard must have made an impression, because the executive made a call and told my father to report to the paint gang. My father was given a brush and a bucket and instructed to start painting.

If it stood still, he painted it. He even painted the huge gas-holding tanks that are several stories tall. He gladly got on a scaffold and lowered or raised it with a twinkle in his eye and joy in his heart. Me? I get dizzy just thinking about being that high up.

The Depression also taught my father the value of not owing anybody money. All too often, he witnessed families booted out onto the street because they couldn't pay the rent or mortgage. He was a real fanatic about paying bills and never ran up a charge account. He just couldn't stand debt. For this reason, we continued to live in an apartment even though he was at the table, pen in hand, and ready to buy a house. He just couldn't deal with the thought of a mortgage. God bless my mother. She never complained about living in a small apartment and was happy as long as we were all there.

Like my grandfather, my father was a union man, but never one of those loonies looking to go out on strike all the time. To put in an honest day's work was all that my father ever wanted to do. He remembered that my grandfather had been fired by one of the gas companies for joining a union, so this may have had an impact on his lukewarm feelings toward unions.

I guess I was thinking about all of this because I was now the same age my parents were when they really became adults and left childhood behind. I wasn't ready to do that just yet, and with that thought I nodded off.

CHAPTER 7

IT'S SUMMERTIME

The summer of 1964 arrived on a Sunday morning. Despite the fact that we had attended Mass the day before at graduation, there would be no getting out of it today. It was no good pointing out that Jesus went to Mass on Saturdays when he was a kid; my mother wouldn't buy it. So, off to church I went.

After church, the guys and I had an impromptu planning session to outline our summer activities. Yankee games, another trip to the World's Fair, Freedomland, football, stickball, and Orchard Beach were on the top of the list. While we talked, Freddie read the *Sunday Mirror*, which had a story about the upcoming Beatle movie.

A Hard Day's Night was set to open in America in two weeks, and movie theaters were going to sell tickets in advance like it was a World Series game or something. We decided that we had better get tickets, as we didn't want to be shut out. It was, after all, the cultural event of the year. After we all went home and got changed into our play clothes, we went directly to the Circle Theater and got tickets for the first show. Our anticipation for the movie increased when all the radio stations began playing the soundtrack. But the movie was still weeks away, and there were other things we had to do.

We figured that Father Dolan and Father Gorman would be taking us to Orchard Beach on Tuesday as they usually did, so Monday would be our day to play football.

Wednesday, therefore, would be a good day to go to Freedomland, and Thursday, the Red Sox would be beaten by the Yankees, so we would go to the game. Friday would see our graduation money run out, and then we would have to wing it.

Playing football on a hot field of tar was not the way they drew it up in Canton, Ohio. The good news was that, because it was summer, there were hardly any cars on the street, so that made for a nice wide, if hot, field of play.

A couple of hours later, some of the girls came by and suggested that we all get together that night. Jeannie said we could come over to her house, and Ro had just gotten the record for *A Hard Day's Night*, so listening to records at Jeannie's was a great idea. The guys were to bring a bottle of soda and a bag of chips, big spenders that we were.

Laura and Kathy were not at Jeannie's, but they were going to the beach the next day with Father Dolan and Father Gorman. We listened to records, danced a little, and had a great time. Summer was only a couple of days old, and it seemed this would be a special summer. We broke up our party a little earlier than usual because we all had an early day tomorrow. I don't know what it is about priests, but they always have to go to the beach at the crack of dawn.

This particular crack of dawn arrived at nine in the morning on Tuesday. We all assembled at the church and walked over to the St. Lawrence Avenue station of the Pelham Bay local. We took the 6 train all the way to the end to Pelham Bay, and then took a bus to Orchard Beach. There must have been about a hundred kids, and no one paid carfare. Anything we had at the beach was on us, but Dolan and Gorman were pretty cool to take all of us. The trouble was this particular Tuesday happened to be my birthday.

My friends had something special planned. They couldn't just get me a card and slip a few bucks in it. They had to be creative. They fashioned a birthday cake out of an order of French fries and stood one of the crispier potato sticks straight up to simulate a candle complete with a dab of ketchup to look like the flame. Then the entire entourage, including the priests and a couple of people no one knew, got into the act with a rousing rendition of "Happy Birthday." It was all very embarrassing, but I was now fourteen.

The rest of the day was spent frolicking in the waters of the Long Island Sound (I did mention that we were with girls, right?) bombarded by the sights, sounds, and smells of summertime that I wished could have lasted forever. However, the inexorable sweep of the second hand transformed hours into minutes and minutes into fleeting moments, and before we knew it, we were making our way up the steps to the 6 train and heading home.

As we waited for our train, we made plans for tomorrow's trip to Freedomland.

In anticipation of the soon-coming World's Fair, somebody had thought it was a good idea to build another amusement park a few years before the Fair would open. We couldn't agree more.

Before Freedomland was built, we had to go to Steeplechase Park in Coney Island to get our thrills on roller coasters and other rides. But traveling to Coney Island was tantamount to going to the other side of the earth. It was a three-hour subway ride, or at least it felt like a three-hour trip. Even though we had a car, my father was always reluctant to drive there.

Our other amusement park alternative was in New Jersey. Of course, we could have skipped the bother and fuss and taken the public service bus to Palisades Amusement Park, but Coney Island was a favorite spot for my parents. For me, Freedomland was ideal because it was in the Bronx, and no mind-numbing trip was required.

The cool thing about Freedomland was that, although it was built to resemble America in a bygone age, it was brand spanking new unlike Steeplechase Park, which was built when Babe Ruth and Lou Gehrig were trotting around the bases in Yankee Stadium. Freedomland offered the opportunity to witness scenes right out of the Civil War. You were subjected to guns and cannons firing at you, and then you could go and try to put out the Chicago Fire. After that, you would run on over to a huge Flying Saucer and watch WABC radio DJs broadcast your favorite songs.

Although the geographic shape of Freedomland was said to resemble a miniature continental United States, I never took the twelve-dollar helicopter ride to confirm this. I took their word for it and kept my feet on the ground and my twelve bucks in my wallet.

On the train ride home from a long day at the beach, we felt just a wee bit sore from being in the sun for six hours, but it had been worth it. We would get to bed early and be up again at the crack of dawn tomorrow for our big day of exploring Freedomland.

This time dawn arrived around ten o'clock. We gathered at Hoch's Corner and made our way to the Pelham Bay line as we had the day before. After a twenty-minute subway and bus ride, we were at the gates and forking over our money as happy as can be.

With the Beach Boys blasting on the PA system, Freddie, PJ, Trent, Mike, and I joined in singing "I Get Around," and we did just that as we entered the streets of America in the 1890s. Since we had more money than we knew what to do with, we thought it would be a great idea just to piss it away, so we headed straight to the arcades.

Freddie was an ace at the shooting gallery, but you couldn't win anything there so we moved on. We found a game of chance where you could win stuffed animals. Five bucks later, we waved the white flag and left the arcade. Trent was not happy. He had a plan.

"Listen, let's go to that water gun game that you shoot into the clown's mouth when no one is playing it, and then we can monopolize it, so one of us will be guaranteed to win." It made sense, so we made our way back to the arcade.

The five of us bellied up to the game and placed our quarters at various water gun spots. Just as we were about to start, another two kids anted up. We all shook our heads at our bad luck, but when the first balloon popped and Freddie actually won, we breathed a collective sigh of relief.

We all agreed on the biggest teddy bear we could get, which we named Bridgette for some reason, and then we identified the second flaw in our plan. Who wanted to carry a fuzzy, stuffed teddy bear in ninety-degree heat all throughout Freedomland? None of us did, so we dutifully took turns.

I didn't know what nostalgia meant, although I think it was one of the Words of Power that Sister Margaret had drummed into us when we were studying for the CO-OP exam. I heard somebody use it as the reason why Freedomland was so popular, and why it was different from the World's Fair. Where the Fair highlighted the world of tomorrow, Freedomland glorified our past.

Of course, there were no expositions about slavery, or about the Robber Barons who beat up workers who tried to form a union. Only good things about the past were on display. No, the American Experience was to be glorified, not ridiculed, which was just fine with us on this hot summer's day. There would be time enough to study that stuff in high school. For now, the smell of popcorn and hot dogs put those things out of our minds.

We spent the next day at Yankee Stadium watching the M&M Boys swatting homers. We cheered and thought about the World Series and important stuff like that. This philosophy would get us through the rest of June and all of July.

—∞—

Of course, not all our activities involved amusement parks and baseball games. Sometimes our week consisted of nothing more than sleeping late and playing stickball and football. Maybe a party or a barbecue would be thrown in.

Occasionally we ventured up to Ferry Point Park, which was under the Bronx Whitestone Bridge, on the Bronx side of course. There, we played softball, skipped stones into the Long Island Sound, and climbed the Big Rock. PJ always said the rock was a vestige of the last ice age. Sometimes there would be a Good Humor man there, and we would get the ice cream flavor of the week. My favorite was coconut, but I also liked toasted almond, though I have never been a fan of strawberry shortcake.

We also packed a sandwich and a soda for lunch. Man, I'm telling you nothing beats a squashed peanut butter and jelly sandwich washed down with a warm Coca-Cola on a hot summer day.

We formed a softball team to play against some of the other neighborhood teams in Blessed Sacrament. The team needed a name, and as we lunched around the Big Rock at Ferry Point, we tried to come up with a name for our team. We thought of the Jets, but that was the name of the white gang in *West*

Side Story, and we thought that would be too controversial, especially since we had a few Puerto Ricans on the team who voiced their displeasure. So we decided to think of a good name that wouldn't be too offensive.

Now we were teenagers and we were boys, and we were normal healthy lads, but I do not intend to chronicle all of our discussions regarding the various topics best left unread by members of my family. So, every now and then, if you think that I have purposely ignored something, you are correct, and that's the way it is. This was 1964, and the Church still had a list of banned movies that we had to check before we went to the movies, and I do not intend to make this list if you know what I mean.

During our discussion about a team name, Freddie called over to Trent, "Hey, T, what do you have for lunch?"

Trent replied, "Gabagool on a roll."

To which I replied, "What the *bleep* is gabagool?"

But Mike ignored my question and jumped right in. "Hey, how about we call our team the Cool Gabagools?"

Even to those of us who had no clue what gabagool was, it sure sounded like a great name, so from that moment on we were the Cool Gabagools.

Our summer was full of playing one type of ball or another, and we had a grand time. Our days consisted of sleeping late, staying out 'til almost ten o'clock every night, and just having a terrific time whether it was just the guys hanging out or if the girls happened to be with us, too.

Jeannie had her Friday Night soirees, but not as often as during the school year, but we still hung out on her stoop or one of the other stoops in our neighborhood. During these stoop moments, there was always a transistor radio providing background music.

We continued to go to Orchard Beach on Tuesdays with Father Gorman and Father Dolan, except when it rained. Then they would take all the kids in the neighborhood to the movies downtown. They paid for everything except our popcorn. On one of these trips, they asked Laura and Kathy to get a group together, and said they would take us all to Lake Sabego one day next week.

I had no idea what Lake Sabego was or where it was, and I wasn't sure if I wanted to make this trip. My comrades shared my trepidation, but the girls convinced us, so we agreed to go. A few days later, Mike, PJ, Freddie, Trent, and I showed up in the schoolyard, and we all looked around as though we hadn't been there in years. Summer was only two weeks old, yet Blessed Sacrament seemed like a foreign place to us, not because it had been so long since we were last there, but because we knew we weren't going back—ever.

When Laura, Kathy, Ro, Jeannie, Theresa, and Diane showed up, we noticed what a big group we had become. How would we all get up to Lake Sabego? Father Gorman had a station wagon, but there was no way it would hold all of us. Our mood of concern soon changed into one of panic as we saw a figure in a straw hat emerge from the rectory. It was Monsignor Hart!

Once again, I quote my father: Jesus, Mary, and Joseph! As soon as I saw Monsignor, I knew what was coming.

Father Dolan and Father Gorman followed Monsignor Hart out of the church, and all three approached us. Father Gorman did the talking. He made it sound as though he was randomly picking people for their car assignments, but he didn't have me fooled. He had this planned all along. "Okay, let's see... hmmm...the girls will come with me and Father Dolan, and the boys will ride with Monsignor Hart."

One of the guys yelled out, "Shotgun!" But I guess he did it out of force of habit, because there was no way any of us wanted to ride up front. It didn't matter. Mike, Freddie, and I dashed to the back seat leaving PJ and Trent to ride next to Monsignor Hart. Now, the thing about Monsignor was that, though he was an excellent preacher, he couldn't drive a car to save his soul. I thought he was going to go through the fence when he backed out of the garage, and then he scared the bejesus out of us when he left a patch of rubber while turning onto Beach Avenue.

Despite it all, we were already having a good time. I had a couple of Tootsie Pops and handed them out. I kept the purple one. We made a bet to see who could get to the tootsie roll center first without biting the candy off. We were all sucking furiously, each trying to win. At one point Freddie wanted to see how I was doing, but I didn't want to lose any time so I refused to show him.

He didn't like that, so he yanked on my arm and the Tootsie pop shot out of my mouth.

I was sitting right behind Monsignor, and as my hand came out of my mouth, a chunk of the lollypop came off accompanied by a large gweb, and both landed smack in the middle of Monsignor Hart's back.

Well, this caused an uproar of uncontrolled laughter in the back seat, and when Monsignor growled, "You're like a bunch of girls back there!" we went berserk. This turned out to be a good way to keep from noticing that he was driving like a loon. Finally, our laughter subsided as we pulled into the parking lot of Lake Sabego.

This turned out to be one of the best days of our summer vacation. We swam for a bit and then we played football with the girls on the sand, in bathing suits, no less, and it was two-hand touch football—sweet Mother Of Mercy! But of course Fathers Dolan and Gorman, dedicated members of the Thought Police, made sure we avoided the near occasions of sin, but they really couldn't be expected to do a good job. When we realized the girls would always be able to score because we couldn't really tag them, we ended the game.

One of the best ways of avoiding the near occasion of sin was by helping with the cooking of hamburgers and hot dogs. That took our minds off two-hand touch football.

It was a beautiful day. I was standing at the shore looking out over the lake and at the trees in the background when Kathy came up to me and said, "A penny for your thoughts." I told her what I was thinking. I told her that this was such a great day, and that we'd had a lot of great days just like this all through eighth grade, but now we would be off to new adventures in high school, and I wasn't sure if I was up for that.

This must have taken her by surprise because she said, "Wow, Jimmy, you fooled me. I thought you were the confident one, the guy who didn't worry about anything, and here you are getting all worried about the future. I'm glad you realize what we had this year, and I hope you always remember it."

I looked at Kathy with different eyes. I wasn't sure where we were headed, but it was likely that we would get there on our own, though I did think that I would always remember what we'd shared together.

With that thought lingering in the comfortable silence between us, we turned around and saw that everyone was packing up and getting ready to leave.

—ᴥ—

Despite my somber moment at the lake, we still had plenty of summer vacation ahead of us. The next thing on our agenda was going to see *A Hard Day's Night*.

It was coming to the Circle Theater, and I still couldn't believe that we had to get our tickets in advance. It was like going to a play on Broadway, which I had only heard about. Even when you went to Radio City, you only had to show up and wait—and wait—to get in. If you were going to see a regular movie at the Circle, the Loew's American, the Rosedale, or the RKO Castle Hill, you just showed up.

There was always a line, especially on Saturday mornings, but you got in eventually. You watched the movie from the part when you came in and then you waited for it to start again, and when you got to the part where you had come in, you left. People would say, "This is where we came in."

That's how we watched *Rodan*, *House on Haunted Hill*, and *Bye Bye Birdie*, all the classics. (There was the time, of course, when my mother and I went to the Paradise and saw *Snow White* three times in a row.) But for *A Hard Day's Night*, we had to be there for the beginning of the movie and have our tickets in hand.

Laura and Kathy were not big Beatles fans. They preferred musicals of a more highbrow nature, so the guys went alone.

I am not sure if I adequately described the way the Beatles were greeted on *The Ed Sullivan Show*. Those of us who watched on TV could hear the Beatles sing because they had microphones, and they were broadcasting out of the theater. However, if you were in the theater, I couldn't imagine how you could hear anything but the screech of young girls screaming and crying. I was hoping this would not happen in the Circle. I was seriously disappointed.

We got to the theater and found five seats together, which was a lucky break considering that the theater was already pretty full. We were in the back, but not in the balcony. It was hard to talk, as the girls in the theater were already getting antsy. There were hundreds of girls there. I didn't see another group of guys besides ours, and I was starting to get scared. This mob could turn ugly. They might come running at us any minute and inflict pain and suffering on us because we dared to not be a Beatle. With that, the lights went out and the coming attractions started.

People were booing the coming attractions and not being polite about it at all. The cartoon was even worse. They were cursing at Elmer Fudd! Finally, the movie started.

The first chord of the opening song "A Hard Day's Night" had not even been struck when the girls started screaming. The screaming never ended. I can still hear it. All I could think was, *don't these lamebrains know that this is a movie, and that the Beatles aren't actually here and cannot hear them?*

Eventually, we got used to the screaming and were able to hear the music and some of the dialogue. We wound up having to stand through most of it because everyone around us was standing, and we didn't want to be seen as being unappreciative of the Beatles' talent. So, we stood and we danced, and we had a pretty good time all things considered. The movie ended, and we all thought it was terrific except for the screaming. Oh yeah, there was screaming *in* the movie, too.

We sat down when the credits came on and decided to stay for another showing. Maybe this time they wouldn't be screaming so much. Then, just as we were getting comfortable, the matron walked down the aisle. Now, movie matrons were feared almost more than nuns were. They had the absolute power to kick you out of your seat for no apparent reason; just being there was enough to piss them off. They always used to make us move to the children's section right after we had just paid for an adult admission. I thought this is what she had on her mind. I was wrong.

"All right, now, you'll be on your way me buckos." Why were the matrons always Irish biddies, as my mother called them? As we protested, the lights went on, the curtain was drawn, and it looked like they were getting ready to close for the night. The only problem was it was three in the afternoon. She went on. "Your ticket only allows you to see the movie once, so off with you now and be quick about it."

We were dumbfounded. This was not Radio City. I knew that because the bathrooms reeked to high heaven and your feet stuck to the floor. Who do they think they are? Well, we tried hiding out in the reeking bathrooms, so desperate was our mission to see the movie again. The trouble was that they had a guy come in and kick us all out. We were escorted out the door and into the bright sun and sultry heat on this otherwise fine July day. But we had seen the Beatles.

We walked down Virginia Avenue toward Gleason. We were going to go back to Thieriot and get a game of stickball going. First, we had to get a bat and miraculously a mop presented itself, so Trent copped it, and now we had half our equipment. When we got to Gleason and White Plains, PJ went into Lou's, the alternative to Hoch's (I always thought that would be a good name for it) and bought a Spalding. It was a quarter now, but PJ handled the purchase without the rest of us financing it. He chose a good one.

We needed another guy so that we could have even sides. Luckily, George was walking his dog on Underhill Avenue and we told him to hurry. As we waited for George we chose sides, and it wound up being Mike, Trent, and me against Freddie, PJ, and George.

Mike pitched, I caught, and Trent played outfield. Mike had this goofy wind-up he called the Froggy. Well, it did seem to work as the guys had a hard time picking up where the ball was coming from. They went down pretty quietly. Then we were up at bat.

Mike was chosen to lead off. He started to bat as a lefty. I shouted out, "Whaddya doing? You're not a lefty."

He replied, "I have a bad eye, and I see better batting lefty."

"Why don't you go and get glasses?"

"Why? I can hit lefty."

We played. We hit. We pitched. We caught. I don't know if we won. We just had fun, but it was really, really hot, and we sweated like pigs.

So, just as we were finishing the game, who should emerge from Laura's house but Laura and Kathy. They seemed happy to see us at first, but when they saw our condition, they knew better than to come too close. They did come close enough for a conversation, so we asked them where they were off to. They said they were doing work for the Legion of Mary. We didn't know what the Legion of Mary was, and, frankly, I wasn't too eager to find out. But Professor O'Connor couldn't resist.

"So, what is this Legion of Mary? It sounds interesting," he asked. I was dumbfounded. It sounds interesting? Well, the girls seemed delighted to tell us all about the Legion of Mary and asked if we would be interested in joining.

Mike just couldn't contain himself, and I seriously started to question his sanity. "Mr. Newell and I were just talking about how we needed to get involved in something, something that would be good for our souls," Mike said. I looked at him as if he were mad, and he started to look like Jimmy Cagney in *White Heat*—really crazy and wild-eyed, you know?

Well, this was music to Laura and Kathy's ears. Kathy was bubbly at this news and invited us to the next meeting, which just happened to be that night in the church chapel at seven. With that, the girls left us, and I was stunned at the sudden turn of events.

"What the…what did you just do?" I shouted. "The Legion of Mary?" (I have purposely left out all profanity and other topics of interest because as I said earlier, I know my mother will be reading this, and my brother Michael as well, and I don't need any grief.)

"Jimmy boy, you don't have to thank me. I know it's a stroke of genius."

"Oh, it's a stroke all right."

"Look; what's our number one desire? To spend time with the girls, right? So, this here plan of mine will do exactly that, *and* it will show a religious side to us that the girls will just eat up."

I had to admit that he had a point. The point, however, was lost on Freddie, Trent, and PJ, all of whom were having a good laugh at our expense. We decided it was a good time to head home and get ready for the Legion of Mary

CHAPTER 8

DESPERATE TIMES

We decided to dress a little better than we normally would have done if we were just planning to hang out on the corner. We also took showers. I got to Hoch's around 6:30 p.m., and Mike was already there, scanning the newspapers. He talked about this quarterback from Alabama who he thought was pretty good. "Okay, great, that's nice that this Joe something is a good quarterback, but what are we going to do tonight?" I interrupted.

"Be cool Jimmy boy," he said in a singsong voice.

"All right, let's get this over with," I said, and we headed for the church. The one good thing is that we knew we had to see Laura and Kathy because they were getting us into this thing. We waited for them on the corner of Thieriot, and they were right on time.

I think they appreciated the fact that we were dressed up and cleaned up too. I think it was appreciation, but maybe it was relief. Anyway, we headed to church and were soon in the chapel with about ten other kids, all of whom looked really pathetic.

The meeting started with a prayer, and then the guy in charge made note of Mike and me and welcomed us to the Legion of Mary. He told us what it was about, and I know I will go to hell for thinking this, but if I could have run out right at that moment, I would have.

Kathy or no Kathy, no girl was worth this. Don't get me wrong, I pray and I go to church and all, but this sounded more and more like a lunatic group. The first topic on the agenda was proselytizing—whatever that was. We soon found out.

The guy came out with this big red box on wheels, and he opened it up to reveal two doors containing shelves on the inside. On the shelves were leaflets containing, you guessed it, religious information about The Virgin Mary and how to become a Catholic. Next, he took out a big calendar, and he asked who would volunteer to sign up for something.

I was in a state of shock because it seemed to me that he was asking us to take this big red box on wheels and hand out the stuff at the subway station. I must be wrong!

Mike and I looked at each other, and I saw the tiniest bit of doubt in his eyes, which got me very nervous. All of a sudden, Kathy stood up and volunteered that she and Laura would take tomorrow night at six because of all the people who would be coming home from work at that time. This seemed to please the leader.

With that, Mike bolted up and offered, "Jimmy and I would like to join Laura and Kathy." Well, this was just what the doctor ordered, at least as far as Laura, Kathy, and the leader guy were concerned. The leader thought it was a great way for Mike and me to learn how to proselytize. I thought it was a great way to give the guys something more to laugh about.

The meeting broke up, and the girls said they were staying behind to talk to the leader. I didn't really care; I just wanted to get out of there.

As soon as we got out, Mike went on the defensive. "Look; we want to spend time with the girls, and this is a way to do exactly that. Besides, it couldn't hurt to show them that there is something more to us than charm and good looks." I had to agree with that.

Just as I started to calm down, the girls caught up to us, and they were looking happy, sort of, but Laura looked a little weird, and Kathy had a hard time looking me in the eye. Something was up. Yeah, something was up, all right, and we found out when we showed up at the church the next night.

Again, Mike and I were dolled up. You couldn't convert anyone if you looked like a slob, so we played the part. Not for nothing, but we do look pretty good when we get cleaned up.

Mike and I were feeling a bit anxious, I guess, so we got there a little early. We were waiting patiently for the girls, and as it got close to 5:30 p.m., I started to get suspicious that something was brewing. We waited and waited, and finally, the leader showed up with a set of keys. I never like seeing people with keys. He approached us and said, "Okay, let's get going."

I said, "Shouldn't we wait for Laura and Kathy?"

"No, they're not coming," he replied.

I looked at Mike, and we both knew we had been had.

"Whaddya mean they're not coming?" Mike shouted.

Leader guy matter-of-factly replied, "They had something to do, and thought you guys could handle it alone."

"This is Laura's fault," I accused.

"No, this is Kathy's doing," Mike retorted. It didn't matter, as Leader Guy shut us up and gave us the keys to the big red box and told us to get over to the St. Lawrence station and give out the pamphlets.

We took turns wheeling this big red box, and we got to the station just as an uptown local was pulling in. Fortunately, my father and other people who knew me would be getting off at the next stop, East 117th Street, Parkchester, but it was still humiliating to be seen by anyone. We agreed that we would do this for an hour and get the heck out of there, and we would never talk to Laura and Kathy again.

—~—

The next day Mike and I were still fuming over the episode of the Big Red Box. "After all, they knew we were only volunteering to hand out the stupid leaflets because they were going to be doing it with us," I ranted.

"Yeah, who in their right mind would do that except for a woman," Mike agreed. The two of us continued along these lines for about an hour when who should we see walking toward us up Thieriot Avenue?

"Well, well, well, look who's here, Jimmy. You remember Laura and Kathy?"

"I sure do, Mike. Aren't they the two girls who stood us up yesterday and made us look like religious, fanatic fools?"

"Right you are, Mr. Newell."

The funny thing is the girls didn't seem to be affected one bit by our remarks. In fact, Kathy just asked if she could talk to me in private.

"Jimmy, can we talk?"

"Watch yourself, pal," Mike said.

I walked over to her, and together we walked a little farther away from Mike and Laura. Mike was so mad that he wasn't even looking at Laura. I looked at Kathy, but I wasn't happy, and I made sure I didn't say anything.

"Look, I have something to say to you," Kathy started. Something came up yesterday, and I couldn't make it. I needed Laura to be there as well."

"Be where?" I asked.

"Well, I had to be at a family meeting."

"Okay," I responded, but I really didn't think it was, and what else was there to be said? In my mind, she had to do something, and that was that. The fact that she hadn't had the courtesy to tell us ahead of time was something I needed to get over. Kathy could read my mind, so she explained further, though the explanation did not make me feel better at all.

"Look, Jimmy, I'm moving." All of a sudden, I had a very bad feeling. She wouldn't be making such a big deal of this if she were moving around the corner. I gave my standard reply of "okay" and waited for her to say more.

"No, Jimmy, it is anything but okay. I'm moving to California."

I thought of many things to say instead of okay, most of which were words you had to confess when said. I didn't say them, but I thought, *shit*, *sonovabitch* and *damn*.I mean if you're going to hell, it might as well be worth it.

Again, Kathy could read my mind, and she tried to console me. But before she could get a word out, a car pulled into the parking place near us, and the Dixie Cups were singing on the radio about a summer romance. We both looked at each other and laughed. Suddenly I wasn't mad about yesterday. In fact, I wasn't even thinking about yesterday. I was thinking about today and all the tomorrows that she would be somewhere else, three thousand miles away. She read my mind again.

"I'm going to be moving in August so that I can get registered in a high school out there, so we have some time." Right then, I made a promise to myself that I would not do anything to make the next month unpleasant. I would, however, do everything I could to make it memorable.

After the Conversation, as I came to refer to it, we made our way back to Mike and Laura, who still were not talking to each other. I told Mike what was going on, and he patted me on the back and said, "Don't worry, Jimmy Boy, we'll bounce back."

I said, "What do you mean we'll?"

"Look, I can understand why Kathy wasn't there and why she didn't let us know, but that doesn't explain what Laura did." He had a point, but I was still trying to be the peacemaker. Finally, he relented and said, "Okay, I'm doing this for you, but you owe me. Once Kathy is outta here, so am I, with Laura that is. You and I are lifers."

—ʊʊ—

Over the next couple of weeks, the four of us continued to hang out. It was funny, but since the moment Kathy told me that she would be leaving, we actually saw each other more than we had in the entire year of eighth grade. We went to see *A Hard Day's Night* again, we went on a picnic, and we had several parties at Jeannie's house including a barbecue. But eventually, it all came to an end, and she was really leaving.

When Kathy first told me that she was moving to California in August, I was thinking she meant August 31st. Unfortunately, it was much sooner than that. In the last week of July, she told me that she would be moving the next week. I thought those swear words again and made plans for Confession. I told her, "Hey, I'm only fourteen. I don't know what to do or say."

She replied, "Why don't you just say what you feel, but be careful; I don't want you to have to go to Confession twice."

I laughed and said, "Don't worry. I made an appointment for the next five weeks. I think that should be enough to get me through this."

We both laughed, and that made it all good. I wasn't nervous, and I wasn't upset anymore, so I was able to say what I really wanted to say. I hoped it would be something that we would be able to remember fondly in the months to come.

I said, "You know, back on the first day of eighth grade, all I could think about was the Yankees and the Giants, and then I saw you with Laura that first Friday. I think it was September 13th."

"You remember the date?"

"Yeah, I even remember what you were wearing."

"Well, that's no big thing. I was wearing my Blessed Sacrament uniform after all."

"Maybe, but I never saw anyone look so beautiful in one of those uniforms."

She was stunned, but I continued. "I had seen you hundreds of times before. I remember making mud pies in your backyard before we started first grade. But that day, September 13, 1963, it was like I saw you for the first time, and all I could think about was how beautiful you looked."

"So, that's when you first thought of me in a romantic way?" she asked.

"From that moment on I could think of nothing else."

There wasn't much more that needed to be said, by me anyway. I wasn't sure how she would react to my heartfelt confession, but it didn't take her long to respond. She looked at me and said in a very serious, quiet voice, "Let's make a vow that we will always remember being thirteen."

I said, "Okay, but aren't we fourteen now?"

"Yes, we are now. But I would prefer that we remember being thirteen and dancing in the dark at Albert's party. Can we remember that?"

Well, that did it. It was time for me to be stunned. I simply nodded yes. I couldn't begin to say anything; my throat was suddenly tight and dry, and incapable of uttering any sound.

There would be one more party at Jeannie's before Kathy left, which would give us at least one more chance to dance together. I hoped that it would be one, long, slow dance.

I was not in the least disappointed. We all gathered at Jeannie's the next night. Trent, PJ, and Freddie were there, as were Terri, Ro, and Diane. Mike walked up Thieriot with Laura. It seemed they were now on peaceful terms. Kathy came a few minutes later.

Although it had been a hot day, the evening had cooled off, and Jeannie's basement was nice and cool, so it was perfect dancing weather.

We played our records, ate our chips, and drank our sodas. There were laughs and a few tears. It was hard for me to think of tomorrow because I just wanted to savor tonight. Tomorrow would be here soon enough.

We played the same records that we always played, the ones that I will always remember, the ones that will always remind me of eighth grade. I guess this was my official graduation party, because as soon as it ended, eighth grade would only be a memory, a good memory, but soon it would be time to move on.

As nighttime pushed its way into the Bronx, Kathy's time with us dwindled down to minutes, no longer days or hours. The party was allowed to continue until eleven, which was really cool of Jeannie's parents. I wonder if they knew. Eventually the party did come to an end, and it was time for Kathy to say goodbye.

The girls had no problem crying. It was almost as if they could cry at will. This only served to make me even more uncomfortable. Now I wasn't just saying goodbye to Kathy, but I also had to worry about saying goodbye to manhood if I started to blubber. I didn't cry, but it wasn't because I wasn't sad enough to cry.

All the goodbyes were said except for mine. Kathy came over and said, "Would you walk me home now?"

"Sure," I said. I dreaded this walk home. It was like going to Sister Irene Mary's office all over again. It was the walk home to the big goodbye. It was the walk home to forever.

Life was certainly easier when all I had to worry about were broken taillights and artificial Christmas trees. This adult stuff didn't agree with my metabolism or nervous system, or whatever it was that was making me tremble and perspire.

Reluctantly we walked up Leland from Hoch's Corner and arrived at Kathy's driveway, the same driveway where a big moving truck was to be loaded up the next day. She turned to me and smiled, and raised her eyebrow the same way she did when our pinkies intertwined the day we went to the World's Fair. It's the look I will always remember when I think of Kathy.

Then she turned and walked up the driveway. I couldn't look up and just stared at my feet for the next few minutes. All of a sudden, I was spun around and smacked right in the face. Just as she had done the night of Albert's party, Kathy had snuck up behind me to say goodbye in a more meaningful, memorable way. She kissed me one last time and then said, "Jimmy, you take care of yourself. You hear?" She then went back up that same driveway, and that was the last time I ever saw her.

I wasn't really sad. I mean, how could you be sad after being kissed the way I had just been kissed? Sadness would come later. I didn't feel like going home just yet, so I started back toward Hoch's Corner when something caught my eye near PJ's house. I turned around, and there was Mike, skulking in the darkness. "Whaddya doing there?" I asked.

"Hey, I wasn't going to let you face this by yourself. What kind of friend do you take me for, anyway?"

"One of the finest," I responded.

The two of us made our way to the awaiting throng of the best guys you could ever want as friends. PJ, Trent, and Freddie were already gathered at Hoch's Corner prepared to offer the solace that only a group of Bronx boys could offer.

They broke my balls like it was going out of style.

"So, Okie, how long did she kiss him this time?" Freddie asked.

"Did he set any new records?" Trent chimed in.

"Hey, Bear you gotta calm yourself down," PJ howled.

Oh man, what could you do? I just had to take my medicine, because that is exactly what it was: medicine for a broken heart.

CHAPTER 9

I HATE THAT ROBERT HALL SONG.

With Kathy gone, I spent the rest of the summer playing stickball and football and avoiding the books that I had to read in preparation for high school. Somehow, I just couldn't get motivated to read anything longer than a sports column in the *Daily News*. But my mother knew about my reading assignments and made sure that I completed them. By the time I finished Mark Twain, Jack London, and the other authors on the list, summer was almost over.

You always knew the summer was over when you heard that damn Robert Hall jingle on the radio. Man I hated that song! Damn tormentor of children!

I broke my vow to avoid the near occasion of serious thought by watching the evening news one night with my father. Walter Cronkite was talking about something called the Gulf of Tonkin and a country called Vietnam. I remembered Sister Margaret talking about that place back in the fall, but I was only mildly curious about what was going on there now. It was so far away that it couldn't possibly affect me. Besides, President Johnson was talking now, and I never could look at him without being suspicious. I mean Kennedy was killed in Texas, Johnson's home state, and Johnson always had this sly smile that just didn't look right.

More important to me was how the Yankees were doing. Yogi Berra had been the manager, and there was a story about him berating a player for playing the harmonica after the team had lost an important game. Well, the Yankees were playing badly, so maybe he needed to shake 'em up a bit. I still had hope that they would win the pennant and go to the World Series. I only hoped that they would do better than they had done the year before. But before that had the chance of happening, I had to start high school.

I didn't realize how much I loved eighth grade until the first day of high school. Having had nothing but women teachers for all of grammar school, I now had to get used to men teachers, some of them Brothers. Michael had filled me in on the St Helena Brothers, and I'd heard no good news when he told me about them. Punching, kicking, and throwing erasers were all part of their teaching methods. No wonder Johnny can't read; he's freaking unconscious!

So, that first day of high school was no picnic. I just wanted to make it through the day. If I learned something, well, that would be icing on the cake. I just didn't want to feel Brother Eugene Thomas's garrison belt on my butt. I could do very well without learning that.

But as the day wore on, the teachers, even the Brothers, seemed all right. There was no violence and not even much homework for the first day. That would change—the homework, not the violence. To be honest, I saw a kid or two get the odd punch, but they deserved it. The homework, on the other hand, was out of control.

I skated in eighth grade homework wise. It was pretty easy, really. High school was going to be different. First of all, I was on my own. Mike was at St. Raymond's, Freddie at Clinton, and PJ and Trent were at Cardinal Hayes and Cardinal Spellman High Schools respectively. So getting used to new teachers and a new school was only some of the new fun that I had to look forward to. Sorting through the good guys and the assholes in my class was a new extracurricular activity that I also had to master.

Nevertheless, I was getting the hang of it, and before I knew it, I looked up at the clock and saw that it was only nine thirty in the morning! Sweet Mother of Mercy, would this day never end?

I did get through that first day, and at three o'clock, I ran out of the building to the lineup for the bus ride home. Yeah, no more walking three blocks back and forth; now I had to take a bus. It was a nice bus with green, leather seats; well, they were more like fake leather. It also had a unique air filtration system powered by Marlboros. Everybody and his mother smoked except the bus driver and me. So by the time I got home, I smelled like I had spent the whole day in the Stratford Pool Hall. This did not escape my mother's notice.

"Jesus, Mary, and Joseph," she bellowed as she blessed herself. "Where in blazes did you get cigarettes?" I wanted to tell her that the Bronx in 1964 was not exactly war-torn Europe and that cigarettes and nylons were no longer legal tender, but I thought better of it and told her about the bus and the miscreants that I traveled back and forth with. She checked my breath, of course, but she calmed down and made me take a shower and wash my hair.

After my mid-afternoon shower, I quickly got dressed and ran down Leland Avenue to Thieriot to get a few hours of football in ahead of dinner and homework. Mike was already there with Freddie when Trent, PJ, and I joined them. No one had a football with him, so we had to wait until somebody else showed up. We had nothing to do but compare notes on how our first day of high school had been.

"That first hour was a killer; I swore the clock was going backward," said Mike.

"Hey, at least you didn't have to worry about your life; the Priests at Hayes are freaking nuts," PJ said.

"There must be ten thousand kids at Clinton," Freddie said, while Trent was pretty quiet about his first day.

Not taking silence for an answer, I prodded and asked, "So, T, what was Spellman like?"

He took a few seconds to formulate his reply and then orated, "Not bad."

"Let me tell you about my day then. High school blows!" I shouted.

"Jim-a-a-a-ay, what would Lizzie McHugh be saying after such terrible language?" Mike spoke in a fake Irish brogue.

"Look, I guess I will survive, but I don't feel good about it at all. I felt like a fish out of water, and I think this whole high school thing will be four years of living hell with intervals of a basketball game or two," I said, prophesizing.

I added the basketball reference because one of the things I did learn that first day was that Helena's did have a great basketball team. The only challenge we had to winning the city championship was from Power Memorial, which had this kid, Lew Alcindor, who was seven foot huge. Rumor had it that he used the rim to steady himself when he was slipping on his sneaker! We had a pretty good team, but no one was as big as Lew.

Gradually, we all opened up a bit more about our first day at high school, and the general consensus was that if we were to survive, we needed to keep meeting here every day for football and other group support activities. That was not going to be hard to do.

The one good thing about high school was that our gang of friends grew. Terri's brother Carl was a sophomore at Helena's, and he and I traveled back and forth to school, so he became a natural addition to our after-school football game. Other Helena's guys who lived on Leland but had attended Helena's grammar school also joined us. And the girls brought in a few more members as well. However, since Kathy was no longer around, Laura didn't hang out as much. Mike did not look disappointed in the least, and I felt a little bad about that.

Blessed Sacrament still figured in our lives because the priests still did a lot for us social activity wise. One Friday night a month there was a meeting of the Newman Club, which was a real meeting, but thank God, nothing like the Legion of Mary. We talked about some topics concerning religion and then had a music and snack session afterward.

One of the topics we talked about was the Vatican Council meetings that the church had been having all of last year. I remembered Sister Margaret talking about them, and even my father brought it up at dinner a few times. He had a cousin who was a nun and an artist, and she had designed a banner for the big to-do in Rome. Anyway, it seemed that big changes were coming to the Church.

In fact, in our first day of religion class in high school, I learned that the story of Adam and Eve was really just a story. It never happened! The whole thing was just a lot of BS, or what our Brother said was literary form. On Leland Avenue, if you used literary form, we said you were full of shit. There was no apple! No snake! No naked walking about! I was absolutely flabbergasted. What next? No Santa Claus?

Then, on Sunday, we went to church only to find the priest facing us and talking in English. No mea culpas; no et cum spiritu tuo; he was speaking honest-to-God regular English. Now we had no excuse for not paying attention. I felt as though the very ground upon which I walked was caving in. The foundation of all that I believed and trusted was torn ass under (or is it asunder?).

Who would have thought that all summer long, while we played football and stick ball stickball, skipped stones on the Long Island Sound, and said goodbye to Kathy, the bishops were busily destroying the Church. Oh well, at least I still had the Yankees.

—∞—

By the time October came around, the changes in the Church were no longer a big deal, but the Yankees sure were. They had made it to the World Series once again, even though earlier in the summer it looked as though they didn't have a chance. The St. Louis Cardinals were their opponent, and I would actually be going to a World Series Game!

I always took it for granted that the Yankees would be in the World Series. I can think of only a few times in my life when they haven't been. I wasn't the only one who felt this way. Everyone in the Bronx expected that the Yankees would play in the World Series. Even the guys who owned the parking lots around the stadium believed it. They had signs detailing the parking fees that told you how much it was to park for day games, night games, double-headers, and the World Series. These signs were displayed on opening day.

When I went to a game, I always took the 6 train to 125th Street and transferred to the 4 train up to Yankee Stadium. But I had never gone to a World Series game. That was for rich kids. Fortunately for me, my brother Michael needed a new suit.

Michael went to Howard's in Parkchester to pick out a suit. While he was there, he entered a contest to win a ticket to the World Series. Now, no one in my family had ever been to a World Series game. Who had that kind of money? So, the mere hope of winning a contest caused a bit of excitement at 1261 Leland.

A few days after Michael picked up his suit and entered the raffle, he got a call. He had won!

"Man, how great is that? You'll be going to Game Five of the World Series!" I screamed.

He let me go on and on for a few minutes, and then he calmly said, "No, Jimmy, you'll be going."

I was dumbfounded. I really didn't know what to say. I wasn't surprised, because that was the kind of thing Michael always did for me. He and his girlfriend Margaret would see me on Hoch's Corner with the guys and girls, and he would slip me a buck. He bought me a new transistor radio for no reason at all, but Game Five? I could only muster up, "Wow, thanks."

So on a beautiful day in October, this fourteen-year-old would be setting off to see Mickey Mantle, Roger Maris, and the rest of the 1964 Yankees team play in the World Series.

On the day of the game, my father sat me down and gave me his version of a pregame pep talk. First, he told me what subways to take despite the fact that I had been doing this for years now. Then, he told me not to use the bathrooms for anything other than peeing unless it was a dire emergency. Then he added the Joe Louis-Max Schmeling speech, which I had heard so often I could recite it to him.

It seems my father had a friend who went to the big fight at Yankee Stadium a hundred years or so ago, and he held his ticket out in front of him as he approached the turnstile.

"As he was about to enter the stadium, some bozo came up and snatched it right out of his hand," my father said, lecturing me. The moral of the story was never lost on me, as I have always kept my ticket in my pocket until the very last moment when I needed to show it to the guy so that he could rip it.

On this day of days, I initiated fail-safe procedures and brought a wallet with me and kept the ticket securely tucked in said wallet, which was then inserted in my front pants pocket. All I needed was my Mickey Mantle Yankees cap.

My Uncle Al worked for Railway Express Agency, and Yankee Stadium was on his route. When I was six years old, he made a delivery and asked if he could have a cap for his nephew for his birthday. The clubhouse guy gave him one, and when Uncle Al saw Mickey, he asked him to sign it. This was a real Yankees cap, not some store-bought cap with an ironed-on NY logo made out of cheap felt. This cap had a sewn NY logo and was the real thing. It was unlike anything any kid ever had, and it had Mickey's signature to boot.

When I put it on as I left for Game Five of the 1964 World Series, I could still almost read his name. I guess I wore it so often that it wore away, but I knew it was there.

I left my apartment, and as I did, I sensed the historic nature of the moment. I was actually going to a World Series game! I was determined to remember everything about this day. When I got on the subway at the Parkchester station, I noted the number of the car, 6481. I sat on the motorman's side of the car right near the front door. A man got in at St. Lawrence who looked like a guy that Mike and I had given a leaflet to when we were in the service of the Legion of Mary. I didn't trust him regardless, and I made sure my wallet was safely secured in my pocket. That's all I remember about the subway ride because before I knew it, I was getting off at Yankee Stadium.

I had decided to remain unencumbered throughout the day. I hadn't brought a sandwich, and I wasn't going to buy any souvenirs that I would have to carry around all day. I kept my left hand on my left pocket to make sure my wallet didn't go anywhere, and I kept it there until I made it to the gate.

As I approached the usher who was tearing tickets, I became a little nervous. Finally, I was next in line, and I whisked out my wallet and nimbly grabbed my ticket. It was torn and back in my wallet before some maniac could come by and snatch it right out of my hand. I was in, and now that I was safely within the walls of the stadium, I could relax. I got a hot dog and a soda and headed toward my seat. I knew I was to sit in the reserved section on the lower level. The only time I sat in better seats was when my brother Johnny had gotten them from some guy at work. Today, I had a terrific seat on the first base side.

The only problem was that I was sitting right behind a pillar. It didn't matter; I just had to peak around it depending where the action was. I was just finishing my hot dog when a priest stood in front of me and said, "I'm sorry, young man, but you seem to be in my seat." I looked at my ticket and sure enough, my seat was in the next aisle over. I jumped up and said, "Sorry, Father," and made my way to the correct seat. As soon as I sat down, I thanked God for sending me that priest, as now I had a perfect seat completely clear and free of all obstructing pillars.

The view was spectacular. Just like on Opening Day and Old Timers Day, the stadium was fully decked out with all the banners and flags from the old days. There were banners for all the World Series and pennants that the Yankees had won, and it was just amazing to see all of them. Could they win just one more?

The game started, and right from the beginning, it did not go our way. Although we had a pretty good rookie pitcher, Mel Stottlemyre, the Cardinals had Bob Gibson, who was just spectacular. He must have struck out at least ten batters, and as we went into the bottom of the ninth, we were down two to nothing. But I still had hope because Mickey was to lead off the bottom of the ninth followed by a few good hitters.

Mickey came up to bat, and although a home run would only reduce the lead and not tie or take it, I still hoped to see him hit one in a World Series game. That didn't happen, but Mickey did draw a walk, which was good. Now the tying run was at the plate. Joe Pepitone followed Mickey, and he quickly hit a dribbler just to the shortstop side of the pitcher. Pepitone had never been as fast as Mickey, but he could run. He ran down the baseline as the pitcher made for the ball. There was no way it would be a double play, though, because Mickey was already sliding into second by the time the pitcher grabbed the ball.

From my clear, unbiased view, Pepitone was clearly safe. The umpire, possessing the vision of Mr. Magoo, disagreed and called Pepitone out. Now, why am I making such a big deal over the first out of the inning? Here's why:

The next batter was Tom Tresh. With Mickey at second and in desperate need of a big hit, Tresh came through in a big way. At the crack of the bat, the stadium was rocking. I couldn't believe my eyes. Tresh hit a game-tying, two-run homer. After we had all calmed down, all I could think about was that if that umpire had called Pepitone safe, we would be watching the Yankees mob Tresh because we would have won the game. Instead, we were going into extra innings.

Extra innings was still better than losing, and I could only hope that we could score a run in the bottom of the tenth. The problem was that the Cardinals rookie catcher hit a three-run homer in the top of the tenth, which proved to be the game winner. So, my first World Series game did not turn out so well, but it was still a great game.

That game proved to be the pivotal game in the World Series, though, as the Yankees came back and won Game Six, which forced a game seven. Stottlemyre and Gibson squared off again, and once more, Gibson won, and with that, the Cardinals beat the Yankees, but it had been a very exciting World Series.

This was the first time in my life that the Yankees had lost the World Series two years in a row. Even though this year's had been better than in '63 when we were swept by the Dodgers, it still hurt to lose, especially because I had to watch us lose in person.

CHAPTER 10

DOMINOES USED TO BE A GAME.

High school became less terrible, but I wouldn't say I liked it. I just wasn't interested in school, I guess, or maybe it was because I was in a new place with new people who were not the friends I was used to going to school with. It just wasn't the same. I did try to get involved, and I joined the speech club or Forensics as it was known officially. I was chosen for extemporaneous speaking. When I was told this, I had to look the word up. I would be doing speeches on topics that the contestants drew from a hat.

The idea was that you prepared all week by reading about current events in magazines such as the *US News and World Report*, and you hoped that a topic you were familiar with was snatched out of the hat. I read a lot about Vietnam. It seemed that, since August, Vietnam was getting to be a hot spot, and we were sending men over there to fight.

I suppose that because of reading all this stuff about Vietnam, I grew to understand the need to stop the communists because of something called the Domino Theory. If Vietnam fell, then all the countries in the area known as Southeast Asia would become communist, too. It seemed to make sense. I had no doubt that our leaders knew what they were doing, and to this fourteen-year-old, the communists were still the enemy. Besides, if you couldn't trust your government, whom could you trust?

The election of 1964 had Barry Goldwater running for the Republicans against Lyndon Johnson of the Democrats. I didn't think there was any way Johnson would lose, but Goldwater was interesting to listen to. He was considered a hawk, as in a war hawk, and he had the reputation of being a mad bomber, meaning he would toss nuclear bombs at the communists the minute he was in office. We were never able to find that out, as Johnson won in a landslide.

After the election, I wrote Goldwater a letter as part of a history assignment. In it, I gave him my condolences for losing and said nice things about him. I got a letter from him in reply, in which he stated, "Twenty-seven million people can't be wrong." When I read this, I wondered what he thought about the forty-three million who voted for Johnson. Regardless, only the future knew how many people would or would not be wrong.

I guess even bigger than the re-election of Johnson was the election of JFK's brother Bobby as a senator from New York. During the campaign, we actually got a chance to see Bobby Kennedy in Parkchester, right in front of Macy's. Just listening to him talk, no one would mistake him for a New Yorker, especially in the Bronx. You know how phony politicians can be. I almost expected him to wear a Yankees cap at the Parkchester speech. I guess he either had the good sense to know that we wouldn't buy it, or maybe he just refused to wear the hat of the hated Yankees. That Boston accent was a dead giveaway of a Red Sox fan.

He won and was now our Senator. I figured I'd keep my eyes on him to see if he was just a guy looking for a good job, or if he was really a good guy looking to do a good job.

The election was not the only important thing going on in my first year of high school. There was, of course, the Beatles.

Far from being a flash in the pan, the Beatles continued to make great music. No sooner had *A Hard Day's Night* hit the silver screen than there was talk about yet another Beatles movie. This one might even be in color! But before that, there would be music and lots of it. I only had two albums, *Meet The Beatles* and *A Hard Day's Night*, but I had a lot of their 45s.

The album *Beatles 65*, which had just come out, had a couple of good songs, but then one night during another late-night transistor radio session in bed, I heard "Words of Love." This was a great song by Buddy Holly, and the moment I heard the Beatles version, I couldn't get it out of my head.

I stayed up night after night, waiting to hear it again, but I never did. Weeks went by, and I just never heard it on the radio. I went to Camera Craft in Parkchester to see if they had it, but it wasn't on a 45 yet. Finally, in June, right before finals, *Beatles VI*, another fantastic album, was released, and on it was "Words of Love." But when I first heard the song, I still had a lot of my first year of high school to finish.

The thing about high school was that in addition to having Brothers instead of nuns, we had six teachers, while in grammar school we only had one. Now, I will agree that being stuck with a bad teacher in grammar school made for a very long year, whereas in high school, the odds of having six clinkers were extremely small. I would have to say that most of my teachers were okay, and I did have some regular men teachers and not just Brothers.

I had this one Brother for English who used to say something stupid all the time, so of course, we said it too. He would say something like, "Shakespeare lived in Albuquerque, New Mexico, right?" Then he would answer his own question by saying, "Wrong!"

How would you like a year of that?

Then, we had a history teacher who used to take a free period with me a couple of times during the year to talk about becoming a Brother. I used to tell him, "No offense, but if I'm going to give up...you know...everything, I'm going to be a priest and say Mass, consecrate the host, you know?" He stopped taking me out of class after a few sessions.

Our science teacher was a whack. He hit me in the face with a blackboard eraser. To be fair, the kid he was throwing it at ducked, so it hit me. The jerkface drew blood and didn't even say he was sorry or that I could go get a drink of water or something. Then when some kid acted stupid, he would come around from the back and demonstrate inertia with this gargantuan college ring. He'd turn it around so that the stone was palm side up. Then he'd put his hand behind the offending student's head and say, "A body at rest tends to remain at rest unless acted upon by an outside force." Then *whack*! He'd smack the kid in the head with the ring. Higher education was amazing. I guessed that college professors probably shot their students, if the teacher violence in high school was any indication.

I don't know why I really didn't enjoy high school. I guess being threatened six periods a day didn't motivate me to want to study. I just wanted to survive. On top of it all, I had just come out of eighth grade where we were the kings of our school. We were the oldest, and the nuns, priests, and teachers treated us really well. Now here I was back where I had been in first grade, and I had no Miss Gallo to look out for me. But life goes on, right?

Blessed Sacrament continued to be a place for us to return. In addition to going to church on Sundays (well, I went, but I can't say all the guys were steady churchgoers), we had the Newman Club, roller skating trips, and the odd dance or two. But that didn't mean that I stayed out of trouble. They say confession is good for the soul, but I didn't think this was worth mentioning in the confessional. It's hardly worth even mentioning it here, but what the heck.

I still couldn't get over how the school bus was like a rolling ashtray. Seeing all these kids smoking day after day got me curious. I had to find out what smoking was all about. My father smoked a cigar, and my mother, I was told, would sneak the odd Camel every now and then. So, I thought that maybe I should try it. One Friday night I did exactly that, and it was not an especially good experience.

I realized that smoking on Leland Avenue would not be possible. For one thing, there were too many people who knew me, and, more importantly, they knew my mother and father as well. Besides, I didn't want any of my friends around, and I was not sure why. Just thinking about it now makes me feel sneaky and dirty. Anyway, I set out to do me some smoking. I bought a pack of Salem cigarettes at Rajah's, the candy store on the Circle.

I took the pack off the counter and walked up Metropolitan Avenue toward Macy's. I actually went to the back of Macy's where there was a parking lot and a few other stores that were closing up for the night. I spent the better part of Friday night smoking like a chimney. I even took the filter off one to see what smoking a non-filtered cigarette was like. That was my last mistake for the evening.

No sooner had I finished that cigarette than I really started to get sick. I set off for home because I really didn't want to throw up on the street like some wino. I got home, and thank God, my mother knew about the school bus and the smoking because she must have been numb to the smell of smoke on my clothes by then. I got undressed and went into the bathroom, where I immediately got sick. I told my mother it must have been something I ate. No need to tell her that it was a cigarette.

I awoke that Saturday a confirmed non-smoker. Well, I don't count the Tiparillos that Freddie would have us all smoking in the movies, but that's another story.

Later that day, I told the guys about my misadventure, and they were pretty pissed at me. Mike only said, "Smoking's for suckers."

Trent added, "Did you ever kiss a girl who smokes? It's downright disgusting."

PJ couldn't believe I was such an idiot, and on that note, I ended my flirtation with cigarettes.

I still don't know why I joined the speech club. I never really liked getting up in front of the class, and I really didn't have much to say. Despite my reluctance to stand up and speak, I found myself getting up on Saturday mornings, and dressing up as if I were going to school before heading off to some other high school for a speech tournament.

Giving up after-school time three days a week and then losing an entire Saturday was just asking too much of a kid. So I only participated in speech club for my first year of high school.

Playing football on Thieriot Avenue was more important to me than talking about some country I hoped I would never visit. Unlike the previous year, however, I always made sure that I did not throw a football anywhere close to a car. Our group of players did expand during freshman year to include Gary, Carl, another Jimmy, and a couple of other guys. It wasn't too long before we had enough guys to form a real team.

We took this team to play in the playground of PS 125 as well as Soundview Park, which was a grass field. For our football team, we chose a name that we all could agree on, the Falcons, and decided to get jerseys. Now, money was tight, and we really didn't want to spend too much, so we sought out a really cheap sporting goods store to see what they had. Freddie, Mike, and I went over to the Grand Concourse, sort of near Yankee Stadium, and saw a couple of nice jerseys. One was a royal blue with red stripes that looked really cool. The other was a bright orange with black stripes. That one looked really hideous.

The salesman told us how much the jerseys cost, and we came up ten dollars short—a huge sum. However, just as he had done when I was in need of a big donation for my taillight fundraiser, Freddie came through again. This time, however, there was a catch.

Freddie offered to chip in the extra ten dollars, but only if we got the orange jerseys.

The first time we wore the jerseys was for a game with some guys that Mike worked with at a supermarket. When we walked onto the field, his boss yelled out, "Hey, Mike! I thought your team was the Falcons. You look more like pumpkins." Fortunately, we won the game.

After our first win in our new jerseys, we decided to meet up after we washed up. We had a new meeting place to go to on Westchester Avenue under the EL. Sorrento's was a pizza parlor where you could sit in a booth, eat your pizza, and listen to the jukebox. We all told our mothers that we would be going out for dinner, which always resulted in a half-hour argument. After those festivities, we found ourselves on Hoch's Corner at around seven o'clock.

We made our way to Sorrento's, and as we walked in, Anita, the waitress, called out, "Hey, Tony, don't worry, the big spenders are here."

"So, what'll it be, boys? Oh, wait; let me guess. One pie cut into eight slices with eight waters and change for the jukebox."

I guess we were developing a reputation.

"Hey, Anita, don't we always tip you?" Mike shouted back.

"Yes, you do, and let me tell you, that quarter comes in real handy at the supermarket."

With that exchange of witticisms over, we decided to settle down to do some serious talking. Football was the topic, as it usually was, and even though it was summertime and baseball was in season, football was more important to us. The Yankees were not playing too well, and it looked like the end of Mickey Mantle's career was coming. In fact, the Yankees were going to have a Mickey Mantle Day in September, and I still needed to get a ticket for that.

PJ, Mike, Trent, Freddie, Carl, Gary, the other Jimmy, and I sat down to the project at hand: dissecting our game that day and looking for ways to play better next time.

Mike turned to me and said, "Well, for one thing, buddy boy, you could try throwing more like Joe Namath."

"Who's he?" I asked.

"Oh, come on, he's the QB from Alabama that the Jets have drafted."

PJ said, "Yeah, I was reading something about him in *Playboy* last year where they said he might even be able to throw better than he runs."

"You were reading what in where?" I shouted. "I thought we had a rule about sharing."

"Sorry, Nude, but I didn't want to corrupt you," PJ replied.

Then we changed the conversation back to my shortcomings as a quarterback.

Later that night, a few minutes after I'd returned home, my brother Michael also came home. He and I were big football fans and followed the Giants and Notre Dame, so I asked him about this guy Joe Namath.

"Yeah, I've heard of him. In fact, a couple of the guys from the office are getting season tickets for the Jets now that they will be playing over at Shea."

"Really? You're going over to the new league?"

"Sure, why not? It's impossible to get a ticket for Giants games. You practically have to inherit them. This way we will see exciting games in the AFL, and now we have a great quarterback who should really be something to see."

Following Michael's lead, I too, became a Jets fan and a Joe Namath fan. Michael, in fact, sweetened the deal by promising to get me to a game to see Namath for myself.

The next day I started reading as much as I could find about Joe Namath, and knowing that I would actually be attending a professional football game this season made it even more exciting. But this excitement started to ebb as the dog days of August came upon me.

One night while listening to my transistor radio (I am not sure why I always heard these songs late at night), I heard a song that sent chills through my spine. It was called "Eve of Destruction," and it was almost like a litany of stories on the evening news or in the daily newspaper. It wasn't a happy song.

It didn't make me want to jump up and dance like "Twist and Shout" did, or to start singing like "I Want to Hold Your Hand" did. It made me think, though, and I did not like what I was thinking.

The world was changing, and it didn't seem to be changing for the better. The previous summer we had still been in shock over the Kennedy assassination. This summer, we weren't in shock, but I noticed a change in mood. More and more stories were coming out about racism in the south and bussing school kids in the north. No one seemed to be happy, and there was no optimism like we'd had when President Kennedy was still alive. Even during the Cuban Missile Crisis, I never felt this anxious. On top of this, it sounded as though the war in Vietnam was not going to end any time soon; it sounded like it was only going to get worse before it got better.

The words of "Eve of Destruction" were as disquieting as they were an accurate portrayal of the American psyche. The lyrics came right off the front pages of the New York Times and summed up what was going on in America.

I wasn't sure if my sense of change was because America was really changing, or if I was just getting older and paying attention to what was going on. I do remember things that upset me when I was a kid, like Buddy Holly dying in a plane crash, Lucille Ball getting divorced from Desi Arnaz, and George Reeves, the actor who played Superman, killing himself (but I still don't believe that). It just seemed that ever since President Kennedy's assassination there had been a lot more to worry about.

—~—

When the second Beatles movie came out, all of this unease quickly left me. *Help* was in color and was just a terrific movie with fantastic songs. "Help," of course, was a great song as well as a great title for a great movie, but "You've Got to Hide Your Love Away" and "I Need You" were just fantastic songs. The Beatles even came back to America, but this time instead of just going on *Ed Sullivan*, they played a concert at Shea Stadium.

That was a great night in August, just a few weeks before we went back to school. We were all excited, and all the guys and girls in our group of friends were there. We almost had to fight for a good seat.

Of course, the seat was on Jeannie's stoop and not in Shea Stadium, but the radio stations were going to be playing Beatles music all night long into the wee hours of 10:00 p.m. It wasn't as good as being at Shea listening to John, Paul, George, and Ringo live, but we all had a great time, nevertheless.

Another British group that was one of my favorites, the Dave Clark Five, also had a movie out that summer. *Having a Wild Weekend* was going to be playing at the RKO Castle Hill, and a bunch of us were planning to go. There was a rumor that the Dave Clark Five would be making an appearance and would sing a few songs.

We had a group of about ten guys and girls, and I have to admit that I was pretty excited, and not just because there was a new girl in our group—a blonde bombshell. Unfortunately, she possessed the stereotypical goofiness of a blonde bombshell, but what the heck; she was still something to look at.

This was another movie where you had to get there at a specific time. I hoped this fad wasn't going to stick, as it was annoying having to know what time a movie was going to start. We showed up with plenty of time for the movie and even managed to get good seats in the center of the movie theatre. But before the movie started, we hit the candy counter, which is where I lost interest in the new girl because she showed her true self.

I was getting popcorn, and she started talking really loud in a moose-like voice. I couldn't make out what she was bellowing, but then I realized that she was barking, "Where's the soda machine?"

Well, she went on and on, and it was embarrassing just standing next to her. Finally, I couldn't take it anymore, and I yelled out, "Right under your left cheek! Your ass is leaning right up against it!" So much for a new summer romance, I guess.

We then returned to our seats, and there was quite the buzz in the audience. The rumors were all over the place. The Dave Clark Five were going to sing six songs, and then it was reduced to three. Finally, it was agreed that they would sing only one song, "Catch Us If You Can," which was their big hit. Then, all of a sudden, the lights dimmed and a spotlight came on in the front and an announcer came out. He bellowed out, "Now, direct from Liverpool, England, the Dave Clark Five."

The place went nuts. We were all screaming and clapping, and then we saw them enter the theater and run down the aisle right next to where we were sitting. They stood in front of the movie screen for a few seconds and waved. Then they ran right back up the right aisle and out the theatre, never to be seen nor heard again.

Quite honestly, after that, I really didn't care much for the movie, and I don't even remember what the storyline was. I am not sure which was the bigger disappointment, the Dave Clark Five not singing or the blonde bombshell not feeling the soda machine under her butt.

CHAPTER 11

ONE BOY'S HEROES

School started before I could even get used to the idea of summer coming to an end. All of a sudden, it was Labor Day, and the next day was the first day of school. Like all first days, I had a hard time getting up and an even harder time getting dressed. It wasn't like eighth grade when I couldn't wait to get to school.

The one good thing about the start of the day was that the guys planned to meet on our way to school. We all took different means of transportation to get to our schools, but we still had to walk in the same direction to get to our buses or subways.

Since my apartment building was closest to Westchester Avenue, we all planned to meet on my stoop. In addition to Mike, PJ, Freddie, and Trent, Carl joined us as well. He was a junior in my high school, and I was a sophomore now.

I don't know if I mentioned this before, but one of the subjects I had to take was Latin, and this year there was a Regents exam that I would have to pass in order to graduate. This was going to be a terrible year.

We met in front of my building and made our way toward White Plains Road where Mike took the 42 bus. The rest of the guys walked to the Parkchester subway station while Carl and I went to take the Q44 bus up to St. Helena's. We really didn't get to talk too much because we didn't want to be late on our first day, but we would catch up later after school.

As I got on the bus, I still felt like a fish out of water. I really didn't like high school. But I felt better when I made my way off the bus and met up with a couple of guys who were in my homeroom last year. We learned that we had the same homeroom this year as well, though many of our former classmates did not. This year was going to be very different because we would be the ones changing classrooms, not our teachers. That meant that we had to do much more walking—well running, really. Many of our classes were scattered from the basement up to the fifth floor, and God help you if you were late. In a way, it did make the day go by faster.

Lunchtime was always right in the middle of the day. We had three periods in the morning and then lunch, and then another three periods until the end of the day. We had gym once a week, and that was more than enough. We had a cafeteria where you could buy your lunch, or if you brought your own, you could get milk or a snack. Every time you walked into the cafeteria, you could hear this old lady screech out, "Hold your milk so it can be seen!"

Naturally, we exaggerated our compliance to her request, and raised our containers as high as possible while adding our own screech: "Here I am, lady! Here I am holding my milk so it can be seen!"

Tuesdays were hot dog days. Maybe the school didn't know that they were made with pig lips and assholes.

Music was often the subject of our lunchtime discussions as sports this year were a bit of a disappointment. The Yankees were not playing well at all, and I was afraid they would finish in last place. The Giants were not playing well at all either, and so far, the Jets were not that exciting, as they weren't starting the new guy yet. So, everyone talked music. The Rolling Stones had a big hit in the summer, "I Can't Get No Satisfaction," which was still topping the charts. A new group, the Byrds, had come out in the summer with a great song, "Mr. Tambourine Man," and it was my favorite at the moment, which was saying something because the soundtrack from *Help* had four of my other favorites.

Despite the fact that I was becoming a bigger fan of football than baseball, one of the most memorable days in my sophomore year occurred at a Yankees game. I would forever remember September 18, 1965 as Mickey Mantle Day.

On a beautiful Saturday afternoon, I, along with a few thousand other fans, went to Yankee Stadium to pay tribute to the Mick. As a team, the Yankees were not doing that well, and I guess the new owners needed a gimmick to get fans to go to a game, so they decided to give Mickey a day. They also knew what we did not: that Mickey was nearing the end of his career. It was the kind of day I would remember forever.

Although there must have been fifty thousand adoring fans, I felt like I was there alone. I was there to honor Mickey, but on this day, I was introduced to the concepts of grief and loss. Sure, the Kennedy assassination taught me about death, dying, and national tragedy, but losing Mickey as a hero was something quite different. After all, I had been a Mickey Mantle fan since I was six years old. So on September 18, 1965, I once again wore the cap that my Uncle Al had gotten me at Yankee Stadium because Mickey was wearing its match.

Listening to the crowd cheer for Mickey and watching him just stand there not knowing what to do, well, all I could do was cheer with them and wonder why I hadn't gone to see more games. I guess I took it for granted that Mickey would always be there patrolling center field like nobody else and hitting mammoth home runs that threatened to leave the ballpark. Now the Yankees were giving him a day because they knew his playing days were numbered. Hadn't it only been last year that Mickey had hit that game-ending home run off the Cardinals pitcher Barney Schultz during the World Series?

It was hard listening to the thunderous ovation that we gave Mickey without shedding a tear or two for ourselves. Seeing your hero get old only serves to remind you of your own mortality, and fifteen is much too young an age for such a lesson.

The ovation was finally over for the moment. The game began, and baseball is baseball. However, when Mickey came to bat in the bottom of the first inning, the ovation started all over again, but this time the opposing team was on the field. I then saw something that I had never seen before.

Not knowing what to do because of the long ovation for Mickey, the Detroit Tigers pitcher stepped off the mound and headed to home plate. When he got there, he stuck his hand out to congratulate Mickey. It was really nice to know that this player and the Detroit Tigers appreciated the Mick and had a deep appreciation of baseball and his place in its history.

It wasn't too long before I realized that heroes—like girlfriends—come and go. It doesn't mean that you ever really forget them, only that you have to move on. It's nice to know that there are a seemingly limitless number of replacements for both. Remember them all. Remember there will be another one around the corner to take the last one's place. You will never run out of either to worship and adore.

When I got home from the game, my brother Mike informed me that I was to see my first Jets game later in the season. I would get to see the rookie quarterback that everyone was talking about, Joe Willie Namath. The Lord taketh away, and the Lord giveth.

Fall was upon us in earnest, and as soon as there was more than a hint of a chill in the air, I began to think about the holidays. Unfortunately, this year our Christmas vacation was going to be a short one. It was still only November, and I had a long month of school ahead of me before I could even begin to moan about a short vacation, but then Santa came early.

I was just about to sit down to dinner on November 9th when we lost all electricity. Now, this was a common event, and my father frequently had to go down to the boiler room in our building and change a burned-out fuse. The wiring in our building was not always reliable.

So, at around five-thirty that night when the lights went out, my father went to his stash and selected a fuse. Before he could open our door to head down to the boiler room, our neighbor from across the hall knocked on the door. It seemed that she had lost power, too. My father soon realized that the whole building was dark, and then I noticed that there were no streetlights on, and all of Leland Avenue was pitch black.

My father and I went downstairs with a flashlight to see what was going on. As soon as I stepped out of my building, I heard Freddie calling me. "Hey, Noodles, the whole neighborhood is dark. No one has any power."

We walked down to Westchester Avenue, and there were no subways running on the EL, and there were no signs of any lights on anywhere. This was more than a blown fuse. It was a blessing.

Finally, Mike showed up with a transistor radio and we learned that there had been a major problem, a blackout they called it. My father began to worry about my brother Michael who would be on his way home from work riding the 6 train. Dad went back upstairs to let my mother know what was going on.

Mike, Freddie, and I were soon joined by PJ, and the first thing he said was, "Hey, this is great! I have a geometry test tomorrow, and now we won't have school!"

"Do you think?" I replied.

"There's no way there'll be school," PJ said. "You can't have heat without electricity, and of course there would be no lights. That's a formula for a day off if I ever saw one."

We all agreed with PJ, and when our flashlights started to flicker because the batteries were getting low, we decided to head back to our homes. As soon as I got upstairs, I alerted my mother that there would be no school tomorrow. To my astonishment and great relief, she did not argue. I think she was a little scared by the whole blackout thing; I think it reminded her of the Cuban Missile Crisis. I was surprised that she didn't have us kneeling and saying the Rosary.

Fortunately, the stove still worked, and we had plenty of candles because they always came in handy whenever the lights went out. So, although there was no TV, we were able to eat and play cards on the kitchen table until it was time to go to bed. It was actually kind of fun. It almost felt like being a pioneer or a kid living back in the nineteenth century, except we had indoor plumbing.

We were only into our second hand of Crazy Eights when we heard Michael coming up the stairs. Well, you might wonder how we knew it was Michael coming up the stairs of an apartment building. It wasn't like he could have rung the bell from the vestibule downstairs. No, my mother was able to identify people by their step. She could tell who was coming up the stairs by the sound of their footfalls. I had long ago stopped trying to figure her out, because she was always right.

Thank God, Michael never made it to the subway. He hadn't left work until after six, so the power was already off in lower Manhattan. He was able to hitch a ride up to 180th Street with a friend of a friend, and from there he walked home. The ride home, he said, was really slow due to the lack of traffic lights and the general chaos caused by that, but all in all, he was lucky to get home safely.

—∞—

The next day was a great day. Unexpected holidays are like that. There was football in the afternoon, and by evening, our lights had been turned back on and TV was restored. Unfortunately, I still hadn't done the homework that I was supposed to do the night before. I hated homework.

Later that week, I got another unexpected treat; my brother told me we were going to a Jets game. This was going to be my first pro football game, and I was finally going to see what this guy Joe Namath was all about.

Finally, the big day came, and my brother Michael and I headed off to see the Jets. One of the guys that he sat with wasn't going to be there, which is why I was able to go. I knew one of the other guys there, Michael's friend Al who had come to the house for dinner one night. I was really getting excited as we got close to the Big Shea, as the Jets radio announcer called it.

It was a perfect November day with just enough of a chill to make it great football weather, but not so cold that we were going to freeze our butts off. As we made our way to the seats, we could tell the crowd was looking forward to this game. Namath was finally starting as quarterback, and he had a couple of wins under his belt. I could tell even on TV that he could really throw a ball. Unfortunately, he didn't have great knees, and he was unable to run around like he had done in college.

The seats were terrific, right on the fifty-yard line, but they were all the way up in the upper deck. I was a little light-headed by the time we got up there, but it was well worth it. My brother's friends were all really nice guys and made me feel at home. They even said I was good luck since Namath threw for four touchdowns, and we had a great win over the Oilers. I was now an official Joe Namath fan, and the Jets were my team.

Of course, this was like treason in the Bronx where the Giants and the National Football League were fan favorites. But there was something different about this new league and this quarterback. The players looked faster, and the game was much more exciting, filled with passing and long touchdowns. By comparison, the NFL was slow and methodical and, quite honestly, boring.

Of course, just one year ago, I had been a big Giants and Y. A. Tittle fan, when the Giants were once again in the championship game. But like the Yankees (of course I am forever a Yankees fan), the Giants were on their way down in the standings. So, it became easy to be a Jets fan now that they had Joe

Willie Namath in his white shoes slinging the ball like nobody I had ever seen before. I came home from that first game wearing my green and white Jets stocking hat all ready for Thanksgiving and the Christmas holiday season.

—⁂—

We were well into the Christmas season, and the stores were all decorated with Christmas trees and lights. Although Lionel trains were not as popular a gift as they used to be, Macy's still had a small layout set up in their toy department. All the stores in Parkchester were open late on Thursday nights, so I always made a point of going over there to do a little window-shopping on the inside.

The guys would all meet on the corner and head over to Parkchester right after dinner. This was the only occasion that I ever went out after dinner during the winter. It just wasn't done, but Christmas was always the exception.

I always gravitated to the trains while the other guys looked in other departments. They were more concerned with who was shopping than where to shop. For this reason, they often found themselves in the department for girls and women. It made sense really.

We checked out all the departments including the record shop to see what records were on the top ten. It was amazing that the Beatles were still making records after over two years. Every time an album came out it soared to number one. The Beatles seemed to be getting better and better, and no one was getting tired of their music.

Macy's was a great store, and the managers didn't really give us a hard time except when we used to run and slide on the floor in the basement, something about running into paying customers. I always tried to figure out what the bell tones in the store were about. It sounded like some kind of signal, not a fire drill or anything like that, but I was convinced that it was some kind of code to alert the clerks that someone was shoplifting.

The stores closed at nine o'clock, but we were always on our way long before that. We always had to stop at the Hamburger Express for a hot chocolate, so we made sure to get there by eight. This was a great restaurant. They had a set of Lionel trains deliver your order on little plates that were stuck onto flat cars. A loop of track ran parallel to the counter, and it was so neat to see your burger, or in our case, our hot chocolates, coming down the track and stopping gently right in front of us. I always thought that my brother and I would make good workers at this place.

But now that we were in holiday mode, we couldn't help but look at the calendar and realize that we were getting gypped on our Christmas vacation. We were only going to get six days because Christmas was on a Saturday. It was always best when Christmas Day fell on Wednesdays, because that meant that we would have nine or sometimes ten days off. I couldn't do just six days, and thanks to an Irish bus driver, I wouldn't have to.

It must have been New Year's Eve when I first heard about the possibility of a transit strike. I wasn't one to read the newspapers for anything more than the sports page or funnies, and now that I was no longer in the speech club, current events went largely unnoticed, especially when I was on vacation. But that night, I heard my mother and father talking about the possibility of the subways not running due to a strike, and my father was trying to figure out how he was going to get to work.

He hated driving to the city, but it looked like that was going to be his only alternative. I really didn't think anything more about it until the next day when the new mayor announced that he would not give in to the demands of the transit workers.

The newscaster was going on about how all the subways and buses had come to a halt, and that it didn't look like there was going to be any service for Monday when everyone had work and school. It then hit me like a freight train: I take a bus to school! I take a bus to school when there isn't a strike, that is!

Mother of Mercy, did this mean we might not have school? I got dressed as fast as I could and headed down to Hoch's Corner. PJ and Freddie were already there, and they were whooping it up. Trent and Mike soon joined us, and it was as though we had won the World Series. We could not believe our good fortune. We had bemoaned our fate of having to go back to school on Monday when all of a sudden, there was a reprieve. The warden got the call from the governor, and we were free men.

PJ was imitating the head of the union and yelling out, "Thay'll be no school in the marning, me buckos." What joy! What utter bliss! Then Mike brought us back to earth.

"Listen up, today is Saturday. They could still settle this thing by Monday, and we could have school."

"What a terrible thing to say," I chided. "But maybe we should start a Novena just in case."

You have never seen such a group of teenage boys so interested in current events. In between games of football, we ran to the nearest radio to get an update on the strike, and so far so good. You could also tell by the lack of noise. It was a good sign not to hear the subways roaring by on the EL, and there wasn't a bus in sight.

When it got too cold or too dark for football, we made our way to PJ's basement for a Monopoly marathon until it was time for dinner. Finally, we were told that things were not looking good at all; the head of the union was put in jail. Oh baby, that's the spirit; we were sure to be off on Monday now.

Sure enough, Monday came and there were no subways, no buses, and most importantly, there was no school. The strike went on and on. We actually got to Friday, and there still was no school. We went from having the shortest Christmas vacation to having the longest, and there still wasn't an end in sight.

The next week, however, a universal signal must have gone out to all mothers because, we were all told that one way or another, we had to get our asses to school. It wasn't such a big deal for Mike because he could walk. For the rest of us, it was almost impossible. My walk would be about four miles each way. To my mother, that did not matter. I was forced to try to get to school, and so I did.

I walked with Carl, who had also been ordered to go to school, and as we made our way across Bruckner Boulevard by E. J. Korvette's, a car stopped and asked if we were going to St. Helena's. We said yes and were offered a ride, but turned it down. There was no sense in getting to school too early or too easily. We had to be able to tell our mothers what a terrible time we had walking all that way. We got to school at 10:30 a.m., and half the school wasn't there. Even though Carl was a junior and I was a sophomore, we went to the same class because there just weren't enough kids to hold regular classes.

Because they didn't want us walking home in the dark, they let us out around 1:00 p.m. What a day. When we got home, we told our mothers what a waste it had been, and we secretly made plans to meet at Mike's house the next morning.

The truth was that our mothers didn't care if it was a waste or not. They wanted us to go to school. We said that we would try, but they didn't believe it any more than we did. So, we wound up enjoying the rest of the second week as well. It was the greatest.

But all good things must come to an end, and that even applies to transit strikes. The union and the city reached an agreement, so we had our buses back and school resumed on Monday, but it had been heaven while it lasted.

The rest of the winter was pretty boring. School was a big disaster for me, or maybe I was the disaster. I just wasn't into it. There were these two guys in our class, and they kept swapping places in class rank. During one marking period, one would be at the top of the class and the other would be number two. The next marking period they would swap, and so on.

One time I remarked to a guy in my class, "No wonder they always do so well. I could be up there too if I studied like they do." That's how it was. I just didn't get it. If I didn't get it the first time around, it couldn't be assumed that I was going to study hard and get it later. Of course, I never told my parents that. Although I didn't want to admit it, I knew that if Kathy had still been around, I would have tried harder. Oh well.

Finally, sophomore year ended, but the end of the year did not come without a cost.

CHAPTER 12

I FEEL A DRAFT.

The war in Vietnam was raging. Every Friday night channel five ran a list of guys from the tri-state area who had been killed in the war that week. It took a few minutes to see all the names. I couldn't figure that out. All freshman year I had read the *US News and World Report* to get material for speeches. I thought I was an expert on the Vietnam War since that was all I had read about. I was a patriot. I hated communism. I was pro-war. But with this, I didn't know. I just couldn't stop thinking about all those guys getting killed.

The thing that bothered me was that it just didn't seem like the communists in Vietnam were that big of a threat to us. It wasn't Russia. They barely had a country. It just didn't make sense to me. I wasn't even thinking about the danger the war could cause to my family and me until the night I heard my bother Michael talking to my mother and father. Michael had been drafted.

They weren't talking about that, though. Michael was saying something about the National Guard and that he was going to enlist. He thought that was a better alternative than going into the regular army, so that is what he did, and on June 6, 1966, my brother left for basic training. I couldn't help but think that the day was 6/6/66.

You know, I am not sure what I said when he left. I guess I said goodbye, but for the life of me, I really can't remember. I am not sure if it was because of the fog I had been in for the entire year, and my entire high school experience, in fact, or if I was just numb when he left. Maybe I was just scared. I do know that he reminded me about the Jets games and that I would be going to a few more this season, especially since he was getting married in November.

I have to tell you that there was just too much going on for me at that particular moment. I was adrift. I really was in a fog. I was not coping well, and I never said a word about it because I thought that's just the way it was sometimes.

Then, no sooner had Michael gone out the door than my mother pushed me out of the house—to work. She had spoken to Uncle James about it, and he had agreed to give me a job in his grocery store. Uncle James's store was famous for many things. For one thing, Uncle James could add up a list of prices written on a brown paper bag faster than any moop with an adding machine. "Hammmeno sofeof dsofeof dorudrsoento…that'll be $4.48," he would say to an admiring customer. You never knew what he actually said, but if you added up the prices, he was always right, except that while it took you a minute or two, it only took Uncle James twenty seconds. He also had the coldest beer in town.

So, that summer I worked for Uncle James, but it wasn't an employer/employee relationship to write home to Sligo about. Its demise started on the Fourth of July. I assumed that since it was a legal holiday, I would have the day off. But when I came in the next day, I was informed that, in fact, there were no holidays in the grocery business.

I learned quickly. One thing I learned was that sometimes adults are pretty funny in their own right. Take Otto for instance. Otto was this old guy who my Uncle James took care of. He had a couple of neighborhood guys who he looked out for. It was commonly known that Uncle James was a soft touch, and he lent many a buck to people down on their luck. Otto was one of his regulars.

Uncle James hired Otto as his late man. Uncle James would go home around six, and Otto would take over. Now Otto would come in every day around five thirty and say, "It's really hot out there today. I haven't had a beer in six months, but I may have to have one tonight."

Then Otto would have a cold beer in the back of the store. Night after night, it was so hot that Otto would have to break his six-month pledge. He was right, though. That summer was the hottest in a long time. One day the temperature even reached one hundred and six degrees.

Because Uncle James had a big air-conditioner that kept the store nice and cold, people often came in just to get out of the heat. Invariably, though, they would buy something, so it was good for business.

Uncle James's store was stocked with tons of things you couldn't get in any supermarket or delicatessen. You name it; he had it. The one thing that I just couldn't look at was the blood pudding. It was the most disgusting looking thing he had. It was this big, black sausage, or something like sausage, and just knowing that it was called blood pudding made me gag. It didn't matter because many of the neighborhood people ate up the stuff, so Uncle James had to keep reordering it.

But I guess the most important item Uncle James had in the store was Mike & Ikes candy. These little candies came in red and green. They were like Good 'N Plenty, but were more like Chuckles inside than licorice. The thing that made these special was that Uncle James gave all the kids in the neighborhood one red and one green Mike & Ike whenever they came into the store. You never had to ask, and he never forgot to plop two on the counter for you.

Every time my nieces and nephews came over to visit, I had to escort them around to Uncle James's, and he would load them up with Mike & Ikes and a bag full of other delicacies. Visiting Uncle James was a rite of passage for them, as was my going to Uncle James to get my father Ballantine beer and El Producto cigars. Uncle James was in the good graces of the local authorities, so they looked the other way on such purchases.

Working with Uncle James in that nicely air-conditioned store wasn't the only good thing about that long, hot summer. The guys would get together for a football game in the evening, and every now and then we would go to Orchard Beach with the priests in the parish, but then we got some bad news. Father Gorman was being transferred upstate.

—∞—

All the neighborhood kids were devastated. Father Gorman was a great guy, and with Father Dolan and another young priest named Father Jeffers, we had a great team of priests in Blessed Sacrament. Even now that we were in high school, the Church continued to be a central part of our social lives. Of course, my mother made sure that I continued to go to Mass. The Church had dances and other activities that kept us busy and gave us an opportunity to just hang out and listen to music with our friends. I didn't like the fact that this might be changing now.

It had only been a few weeks after Father Gorman left that Father Dolan organized a trip to go see him. On a Sunday morning, about a hundred kids were loaded into three school buses to make the trip up to Beacon, New York. It was a long trip made even longer by the fact that one of the girls on the bus had a portable record player but only one record. She played "You Can't Hurry Love" by the Supremes all the way up there. I was sure the batteries were going to die, but no; they kept on working and torturing us. I made sure not to get on the same bus with her for the ride home.

It was great to see Father Gorman, who seemed genuinely delighted to see us. We must have really made an impression, because you could see a look of amazement on the faces of the people of his new parish. They had to know they had someone pretty special who could make so many of us want to come up for a visit.

Losing Father Gorman was only one new thing we had to endure. Television was also changing as networks seemed intent on offering the most nauseating shows they could come up with. Each network had a talk show hosted by some lunatic who would invite more lunatics on that he could yell at and embarrass. It made you think that the world had gone mad. There were people who opposed the war in Vietnam, and they were ridiculed as cowards or communists, and anyone from the audience who agreed with them (yeah, even the audience got into the act; it was almost like *Let's Make A Deal*) was made to look like they just stepped off an alien spaceship.

Speaking of alien spaceships, PJ kept telling us about this new TV show coming out called *Star Trek*. It sounded like a real winner to me, and I was sure it would be popular with all the crazies who went on those talk shows.

—∾—

When junior year started, I was actually not as out of it as I had been. I still wasn't what one would call studious, but I didn't hate going to school as much as I had in my freshman and sophomore years.

Also, Michael had come home from basic training. That really perked me up despite the fact that he would be home only for a very short while. In November, he and Margaret would be getting married, and he asked me to be his best man. Once again, Michael let me know how important I was to him without actually saying anything.

Michael never let me think otherwise. When he made me his best man, it was just another thing he did for me and took for granted, like giving me a World Series ticket, buying me a radio, or slipping me a buck or two here and there. I guess he knew what being a big brother was all about, and I guess, if you asked him where he learned it, he would say from his big brother, Johnnie. Well, Johnnie was my big brother, too, but you get the point.

It was great to be a football fan in 1966. Notre Dame had a great team, and for a while, it was hard to determine which team excited Michael and me more: the Jets or Notre Dame. Well, Joe Willie always won us over, but we really loved Notre Dame, too. We watched all the games together either on TV or at Shea.

So that fall Michael and I spent our last few weeks living together in 1261, and I guess I got all sentimental about it. One of our favorite evening rituals was guessing what *Superman* would be about that night. We were big fans of *Superman* and had seen each episode a hundred times. One night I guessed that the show would be about Lois Lane and Jimmy Olsen getting super powers from a pill Professor Pepperwinkle invented, and Michael guessed that it would be about a meteor that was going to crash into Metropolis. Of course, he won. He won every night and loved to torment me about it.

It always seemed curious that he would come from the back bedroom after talking on the telephone extension and pronounce the evening's episode as though he'd had a vision or something. I always suspected that Margaret was reading the *TV Guide* to him, but I never could prove it.

Then, before either of us knew it, it was Friday, November 18, the day before Michael and Margaret would be married. I wanted to commemorate the occasion, so I said, "Well, I suppose this is the last night we will guess which *Superman* episode will be on."

He would have none of that. He got angry with me and said, "What do you have to talk like that for?" That was all he needed to say. I knew he was feeling it, too.

Then Saturday came, and we were getting all spiffed out in our tuxes, getting ready for the wedding, and neither one of us could have been any happier. The one thing that caused a slight bit of regret was the fact that Notre Dame was playing Michigan State for what amounted to the national championship, and we would not be able to see it. But things worked out anyway.

The wedding ceremony was terrific. Aunt Catherine must have pinched my cheek a hundred times, and my father must have said, "Did you say hello to Aunt Catherine?" another hundred times. Then we were off to the reception, where I had to make a toast.

This was the one thing about being a best man that worried me. Nearly two hundred people would attend, and when I made my toast, they would all look at me with anticipation, some hoping I would make an idiot of myself.

I had actually forgotten about the toast when, as everybody was dancing and having a good time, the bandleader announced that it was time for me to make the toast. I got to my feet slowly, desperately trying to stop my hand from shaking. I didn't want to be remembered for spilling champagne all over myself. In fact, I didn't want to be remembered at all, but I made sure that wouldn't happen.

I proclaimed, "I would like you all to join with me now in wishing Michael and Margaret a long and happy marriage." I felt that I just had to add something else, so as I sat down, I blurted out,"...and many children!" Well, that got the crowd on their feet applauding and laughing, which I guess trumps spilling champagne all over my rented tux.

Now that that was over, I could enjoy myself. I think Michael relaxed a bit too, because as soon as I sat down after my toast, he called a waiter over and slipped him a buck.

"What was that about?" I asked.

"I just asked the head waiter to keep us posted on what Notre Dame is doing." Once again, Mike was a step ahead of me.

Unfortunately, Notre Dame and Michigan State played to a six-to-six tie, so the argument continued as to which team was the national champion.

CHAPTER 13

THE SUMMER OF LOVE

Junior year of high school ended with the traditional boat ride to Rye Playland. One Thursday morning in late May, we trundled down to Battery Park where a boat, similar to the Staten Island Ferry, awaited us. Our entire high school boarded and set sail. It was a terrific morning; we passed by the United Nations building, and it looked like it was on fire with the morning sun beaming all over its wall of glass.

When we got to Playland, we did the usual things. We went to the batting cage, played miniature golf, and, of course, rode all the rides. One of our favorites was the motorboats kept in a small lake. They had small electric motors so you could only go slowly, but it was still fun.

Too soon, the boat whistle blew, and that was our signal to get going. This is where my day went bad.

We were only on the boat about a half hour when, sitting in the front of the boat, a few of the guys thought it would be a good idea to throw a deck chair into the water. I am not sure if I mentioned this or not, but I am an idiot. I, too, thought it was a good idea.

Now, up to this point, I had made it through all of high school without getting into any trouble whatsoever. I had never had detention. I had never been hit, except by accident. I had never been given as much as a punishment assignment. Why, then, did I think it was a good idea to throw a chair off a boat? Did I mention I was an idiot? I also think that not having my neighborhood friends around me to slap me out of my stupor had something to do with it.

So, here I was kicking a chair under the railing and off the boat and getting poised to kick another when I saw the guys in front of me look up in horror. Then I heard a booming voice declare, "What are you doing with that chair?"

I turned around and looked up into the very angry eyes of our principal. *Oh shit!* I thought, but of course, I did not dare say it. He then said, "Give me your ID card." That was it. No other words were uttered. The guys around me were as stunned as I, and we said nothing.

When I got home, every time the phone rang, I thought it was the principal. It never was, but the stress that I went through with every ring was severe. I knew I was going to get kicked out of high school, and that would just delight my parents to no end.

All I kept thinking about was this stupid movie *Phoebe* they kept showing us to ward us off sex. This fourteen-year-old girl got pregnant, and she was scared about telling her parents, so she kept daydreaming about how to tell them. In one scene, she came bouncing down the stairs and shouted out, "Mom, Dad, I'm pregnant!" The parents jumped out of their chairs and started hugging and congratulating her. Everyone was so happy for her. This was not going to happen to Phoebe, and it wasn't going to happen to Jimmy.

The next day, Friday, was a killer. Everyone at school knew what had happened with the deck chairs. Guys I didn't even know came up and patted me on the back, some in congratulations, some in sympathy. The funny thing is that none of my teachers seemed to know. At least they didn't let on that they knew.

I kept waiting and waiting for the other shoe to drop—to be called down to the principal's office, but it never came. The day ended, and I got on the bus to go home. Fine, I was going to suffer all weekend.

I did suffer all weekend, and all the following week. Monday, Tuesday, and every freaking day went by without a word about my altercation with the deck chairs. I was going insane with worry. Then, there we were in our last period of the day on Friday, a full eight days after my day of infamy, and just as we were packing up, the voice of God came over the public address system. "Will James Newell please report to the principal's office immediately after the dismissal bell."

One by one, the guys came up to me to wish me good luck. Once again, I felt like Jimmy Cagney going to the chair. Bless me, Fadder!

I went down to the principal's office where I was told by the secretary to take a seat. The dismissal bell rang at 2:15 p.m., and it was now 2:20. I sat until three o'clock. I sat until three thirty. I sat until four o'clock. I sat until four thirty. By then, I was completely out of my mind. Finally, the principal came out and told me to come into his office. *Sweet Mother of Mercy*, I prayed in silent desperation.

He started out by saying, "I've had time to review your record, and you're pretty clean. Why on earth did you throw a chair off the boat?"

Never good under extreme situations, I declared, "The chair was broken."

"Is that what the Newells do with broken furniture?" Jesus, Mary, and Joseph! He was blaming countless generations of Newells for my transgression. That's exactly how my parents would react. I was deader than dead. I would have to renounce all living privileges. Maybe if I became a priest I would be absolved of my sins? Oh, man, I didn't know what to do or say.

After realizing that he had hit a nerve and seeing the shame and remorse in my eyes, the principal handed my ID card to me and uttered words I will never forget.

"I'm going to keep this in your record for one year. If you keep your nose clean throughout senior year, no one will ever need to know about it." I can still remember how it felt to have the weight of a life of eternal pain and suffering lifted off my heart and shoulders. I was free! I thanked him and got the hell out of his office in case he had a moment of lucidity and changed his mind.

—∿∿—

As much as I liked going to Jets games and seeing Joe Willie throw the ball, I also liked throwing the ball myself. Now that we were almost into senior year, our neighborhood football team had become a little more organized. We still called ourselves the Falcons and bought new gold and white jerseys with numbers on the back and all. We also played a few more teams than we had played in the past. Just about every Sunday, when we didn't have a Jets game to go to, we played a game against a local team.

Mike and PJ were really good wide receivers and rarely failed to catch one of my spectacular passes. (I won't go into the number of times they dropped one of my passes.) If they had only been able to catch the lame ducks that I sometimes threw, I wouldn't have had as many interceptions. Trent and Freddie played a great defensive line, and sometimes on offense, they caught passes coming out of the backfield.

We had captains and co-captains, and we held meetings, but we rarely practiced. As Mike would often say, "Whaddya gonna teach me?" I liked the meetings best, as we would often meet at the Hampton House, which was a new ice cream parlor on the Oval in Parkchester.

Life was good, and I had no reason to think it wouldn't stay the same or get better, but I just had to watch the evening news to know that I was only kidding myself.

The war in Vietnam was raging, and there seemed no end in sight. I just couldn't understand it. It seemed we were stuck in neutral. I think that deep down, most people wanted it to end, but no one knew how to bring it about. Too many men had died to just walk away, but then that idea seemed pretty stupid too, because it meant that even more men would die. Vietnam didn't seem to be like any war we read about in history class.

Seeing the war on the news every night was a lot scarier than reading about war in a textbook. The world continued to change, and so did our neighborhood, and it wasn't for the better.

We were a tight-knit group of guys and girls, and we really kept one another on the straight and narrow. We weren't angels or anything like that, and I certainly had my share of events that I wish I could have avoided, but our hijinks were nothing compared to a new bunch of wise guys who had started to hang out on Hoch's Corner, and we did well to avoid them.

These guys were all wannabes. They thought they were cool, and looked down at those who were not as cool as they were. They were what Mike used to call cookie and cake racketeers. I just thought they were assholes. You never saw them throw a ball, and I think if a ball ever found them in its arc, they would duck and cover. They just thought they were so cool, and stood proudly on the corner letting us know just how cool they were. A couple of them were so cool that they got iced. The trouble was that they did have influence on the neighborhood.

It was 1967, and the whole country was changing. Young people were freaking out and parents didn't know what had hit them. Drugs were the symbol of change, and they were sweeping Leland Avenue as well as Haight-Ashbury. Fortunately, I had been exposed to drugs years before. We had a couple of miscreants in our neighborhood who were shooting heroin, and if I ever needed a reason not to do drugs, those assholes were my walking proof.

It was common to see these two guys, Dim and Dimmer we used to call them, staggering down Leland Avenue. Dim was an evil-looking weasel who snarled at you when he passed by. Dimmer was a sap. You could see that he was trapped; he didn't really want to be hooked up with Dim, or on drugs for that matter, but he was an addict, and I guess he had no choice. I really felt sorry for him on a certain summer day back in 1961.

A bunch of us were playing Triangle in front of the johnny pump down the corner from Westchester Avenue right near my house. All of a sudden, we heard a God-awful crash. We ran around the corner and saw a beautiful Chevy wrapped around one of the EL pillars. Dim and Dimmer were in the car. They had stolen the car, because neither one of them could have bought so much as a ham sandwich without begging for the money. Dim crawled out from behind the wheel, but I could see that Dimmer was not so lucky.

Within a few minutes, the cops arrived and were able to get Dimmer out of the car. Blood was streaking down his face. He had gone through the windshield, and he was really lucky to be alive, but I don't think he thought that he was lucky at all.

I can still see him lying there on the sidewalk with a big cop hulking over him saying, "You know, no doctor will want to touch you 'cause you're a bug." This cop wasted no love or compassion on drug addicts, yet I couldn't help but feel sorry for Dimmer.

I also couldn't help but be scared of drugs when I saw up close what they could do to you. That is why I had no use for this new group of wise guys when they came to Hoch's Corner. I had no interest in being a bug.

We stayed clear of these guys by playing football, stickball, and softball. We threw in a little basketball for good measure. We also had Jeannie's parties to keep us off the corner on Friday nights, but on nights when we did venture to see what was going on at Hoch's Corner, we stayed within our group.

It was not uncommon on hot summer nights to be a part of about a hundred kids just hanging out, and most, like us, were good kids. It was the Summer of Love after all, and music blared from car radios and big transistor radios while we just hung out on Hoch's Corner. It was like being at a happening, but we had our own organized happenings, too.

As I said, the world was changing, and changes came to us, though not all of them were something to be proud of. I guess they were all necessary parts of our experience in growing up. It was during the Summer of Love that we were introduced to the charms of the Creature.

—✻—

The grocery stores in our neighborhood would sell the odd six-pack to a kid if they knew their parents and if they knew their parents were the intended consumer. I had been picking up a six-pack for my father at Uncle James's store since I was ten, and no one thought anything of it. We knew that we just couldn't go into one of our neighborhood stores to get beer that we were going to drink, however, so we improvised.

We went out of our way to find a store a few blocks from Leland, and we found one right on Beach Avenue. Now, Beach Avenue was also the block where Blessed Sacrament was, but this particular bodega was closer to Westchester, so we felt it was far enough away not to be a problem. We would often go in on a Friday night and pick up a quart of Schaeffer. I'm not quite sure what we found so appealing about Schaeffer, but I guess it was available and cold. We were also sure to pick up a pack of lifesavers to mask our beer breath for when we went home.

Since they were having happenings out in Los Angeles and San Francisco, we thought we should organize one in the Bronx. We endeavored to have a football game up at Ferry Point Park to be followed by a real Bronx happening complete with adult beverages. Let's just say there was a lot of drinking and no love at all as the girls knew better than to attend an event destined to be a drink fest.

I know it sounds like a rationalization, but we thought that having a few beers was not as bad as popping a few pills or tripping out on LSD, and if we had to face the possibility of being drafted and being sent to Vietnam in one year's time, we had a right to party a little now. We didn't want to be left behind. We wanted to be a part of the change, too.

—∾—

That summer I took driver's education. I learned to drive a car in one of the worst sections of the South Bronx. Going to class every day was an adventure in itself, and driving around that area was a nightmare. The worst part, however, was that my family didn't have a car at the time, so I never had a chance to practice driving with my father in the car as most of the other kids did.

My brother Johnny would come over on Sunday mornings and take me out for a ride in his Rambler station wagon. It had a push-button transmission, so even though it was a Rambler, it was still pretty cool to push buttons instead of shifting a shifter.

Despite all of Johnny's good efforts, I failed the road test the first time out.

There I was driving around Hunt's Point surrounded by trucks and buses, and some idiot decided to back out of a driveway, so I paused to let him out. I thought I was doing the safe and courteous thing. My driving inspector, having been a former Nazi, maybe even in the SS, declared, "Mr. Newell, it is not your job to direct traffic." The language that came to mind would not be something to include in this book, and fortunately, I kept it to myself at that time, too.

That was it for driving and me. I lost interest, and I really didn't want to keep bothering Johnny.

—∾—

Senior year came, and with it Ring Day—the day when we got our high school rings. We also started meeting with our guidance counselors regarding college. I thought about going to college only because the other guys were talking about it. My brother Johnny had graduated from Saint John's, so I thought I would go there. Mike was planning to go to Saint John's, too, but Trent was going to Manhattan, and PJ to Fordham. But when it came time to complete the application, I hit a stumbling block.

Putting in my personal information and family information was not a problem. Choosing a major—now that was a problem. I had no clue as to what I wanted to major in. I really hadn't given it much thought because I hadn't given college much thought. It was merely the next thing to do. It sure beat thinking about Da Nang and the other scenic spots in Southeast Asia.

I had to choose a major before I could mail in the applications, so the only thing I could think of was to call Johnny for some advice. When I called him, my sister-in-law Mary told me he was working. When I said, "So what else is new?" she asked me what I needed. I told her that I was filling out the application for college and didn't know what to put down as a major.

She asked, "What have you done well in?" I told her that I had done pretty well in the history Regents exams, so she advised me to put down history. I don't think she said "Duh," but she would have been entitled to if she had.

That fall, it was football weather at its best, and going to Jets games and playing football every day was just terrific. There was nothing better than playing a big football game on Saturday and then going to a Jets game Saturday night. Mike and I went to see the Jets play the Chargers, and just being at a football game at night was out of this world. We had been to many a Yankees game at night, but football at night was a novelty reserved for the American Football League, and we loved it.

It was a perfect day. I got to throw two touchdowns to Mike and PJ in the afternoon and followed that up by watching three Namath touchdowns at night. Mike was even able to see his idol, Lance Alworth, catch a long touchdown from John Hadl, and it didn't hurt the Jets in the long run. Namath threw for four thousand yards that year, and we looked for even bigger things from Broadway Joe.

We had a full house at Thanksgiving, and Michael and Margaret provided the highlight for the family. Margaret had just had a baby boy, Michael, and he was the star of the show. It's amazing what kids do for a family. I don't think I ever saw my mother happier than when the little ones came to visit. Pop, as my father was now known, also lit up like a kid at Christmas when the kids came over.

In addition to sisters, brothers, nieces, and nephews, Aunt Catherine and Uncle Al came to dinner. Uncle James made his compulsory appearance in the morning complete with a jug of cider in tow. How we fit all these people in our little apartment is still hard to figure out. I think it helped that my parents never seemed to sit down. My mother was always in the kitchen doing something while my father operated a one-man assembly line and carried everything into our living room, which was transformed into the dining room once again.

In the background, Laurel and Hardy were saving Toyland, and Bing Crosby was singing "Christmas in Killarney." The Christmas Holidays had officially begun.

My brother Mike and I had agreed that we would keep our annual tradition of putting up the trains on the day after Thanksgiving, so the next day we did. Every time we set the trains up, we observed our annual ritual of retelling the story of how our father gave us our Lionel trains.

Before I came along, Michael had been given a set of American Flyers, and he was hooked on trains from that first Christmas. A few years later, when I was in Macy's—I might have been six years old—I saw a set of the Lionel Santa Fe Super Chief. This was a magnificent train with the huge Santa Fe diesels pulling a set of gleaming aluminum passenger cars.

I was adamant that this was what Santa should bring me that year. I can only imagine the look of horror on my father's face when he saw the $100 price tag.

That year I, too, got a set of trains, and they were American Flyers like Michael had. It was a great set, and I was extremely happy with it. Nevertheless, when I was nine, my parents picked me up at school one day when it was close to Halloween. We were supposed to be going shopping, but when I was getting into the car, my father pointed to the back seat. On the floor was a set of Lionel Trains in a big box.

Well, I was floored and exasperated all at once. I was delighted to finally have Lionel trains, but how could I wait until Christmas to even know what I had?

My father did not intend to have me wait, because as soon as we got back to Apartment 6, he opened the box to show me.

It was a small steamer with the newest cars that Lionel had come out with, including the missile-launching car and the giraffe car. It also came with the dispatching board and a set of trestles so that you could make a figure-eight layout. No sooner had we had the trains out of the box than we were heading into our front bedroom where a table had been set up, and on it, a sheet of plywood had been placed. My father and I laid a sheet of grass paper on it, and then we set about putting up the trains. My father couldn't wait until Christmas, and I was sure glad of that, but it didn't end there.

About a week before Christmas, my father came home from work with a small box under his arm. He had that look he would get when he had something to give you that he was so excited about that he was about to burst until he gave it to you. He told me to come into the bedroom, and he opened the box to reveal a shiny red and silver Santa Fe diesel. I finally had my Santa Fe.

I don't think I had it on the tracks before I put on my coat and ran around the corner to Uncle James's where Michael was working, and I blurted out that we had a Santa Fe. Michael was as stunned as I was. To this day, I am not sure what surprised us more: getting the locomotive in the first place, or our father being unable to keep it until Christmas Day.

When Michael came home, he reconfigured the layout. Since we had two locomotives, we could now run two sets of trains. He completed the redesign in no time, but then we realized that we really didn't have enough cars to run two sets. Michael and Margaret had a plan, though.

Finally, Christmas morning arrived, and Margaret came over for breakfast after church. We immediately set to the task of ripping open the presents, and with Bing and Johnny singing in the background, I opened my first gift from Michael and Margaret. It was a beautiful Lionel Milk Car. Now we were going places, but it didn't end there.

The next day, Michael, Margaret, and I set out to Macy's in Herald Square on 34th Street to do some day-after-Christmas shopping and to see their train layout. Although Macy's in Parkchester had a fantastic layout, it couldn't compete with the Herald Square store. Along with just about everything else in the store, trains were also being sold at reduced prices. It was a bonanza!

We got a beautiful log car, the Allis-Chalmers condenser car, a barrel loader, and a helium tank car that usually came with three helium tanks, though somehow, Margaret was able to convince the clerk that they actually came with six. Let's leave it at that, shall we?

So now, eight years later, as we acknowledged our family train history, Michael and I put the table together and slid the sheet of plywood on top in preparation for setting up this year's installment of the Newell Train Show.

We had the trains up and running and, before we knew it, Christmas Circa 1967 had come and gone.

—
~~~
—

My last semester of high school began and ended when the postman made his appointed round to 1261 the day we returned to school after the Christmas break. With that morning's delivery came my acceptance letter from Saint John's University.

What else needed to be accomplished? I was ready for college, and high school was just a memory still in progress. No sense getting too worked up about high school issues when I was so close to being a college man. Well, that was my mindset, and it was set like concrete.
~~~

CHAPTER 14

WHAT'S GOING ON?

To be fair, there were enough reasons to cause me to be so cavalier about school. The world had elected to self-destruct. The war in Vietnam was out of control. What was being called the Tet Offensive had exploded on the scene causing many to question our participation in the war. Many wanted us to get out, and there was no doubt that the war was going to be the decisive issue in the upcoming presidential election.

Our history teacher, who was also the science teacher who had hit me in the head with the eraser in my freshman year, speculated as to whether President Johnson would even run for a second term. This proved to be prophetic, because a few months into the election season, Johnson announced that he would not seek, nor accept, the nomination. This would have been the most noteworthy event of the year had it not been for two others that dwarfed it in importance and historical impact.

Martin Luther King was an ordained minister and a civil rights activist who was a savior to many and a threat to others. I remember back when Kennedy was president, King had led marches and given speeches that were impressive, no matter what your views on civil rights were. He gave a speech in front of the Lincoln Memorial, and I remember thinking that he was right, that we all should be equal. How could you be a Catholic and not believe that? How could you be an American and not believe that? Unfortunately, too many who considered themselves good Christians and good Americans found a way not to believe that.

So, in April of 1968, as I was typing something for school, I was not totally surprised when I heard the news that the Reverend Martin Luther King Jr. had been assassinated in Memphis. I was not surprised because it was just what could be expected during these terrible times.

I remember how it was when Kennedy was assassinated and how it would have been if he had been killed by any of our enemies. There would have been total agreement throughout the land that revenge for the act must be our goal. Wouldn't Negroes feel the same way now? Wouldn't they feel that White America was their enemy? I was scared that I would be lumped into the group that hated Martin Luther King because I happened to be white. I now understood how prejudice and hatred worked.

There were riots and violence, but most tried to remember the things that Dr. King stood for, and most just hoped that we could learn to live with respect if we could just survive this national tragedy. Then we were dealt another blow.

When President Johnson announced that he would not seek a second term, New York Senator, Bobby Kennedy, announced that he would run. I was excited by this. I had been reading up on Kennedy since he had first been elected Senator, and I liked the things he stood for. I guess the fact that he was the brother of a beloved president who had been taken from us influenced me as much as what I had read about him.

Others were excited as well, and it looked as though he was going to get the Democratic nomination. I went to bed the night of the California primary knowing that he had won, and by doing so, he just about had the nomination sewn up. However, the following morning I was brought back to a day in 1959.

On February 3, 1959, my mother woke me up for school by telling me that Buddy Holly had died in a plane crash. We both loved Buddy Holly, and my mother especially loved his new song, "It Doesn't Matter Anymore." I was nine years old, and it was a terrible introduction to loss.

So it was on that day in June 1968, as my mother woke me up by telling me that Bobby Kennedy had been shot in California, that I just wanted to roll over and not have to face what had just happened.

All I could think about was how such good men could be torn down for the things they believed. Both King and Kennedy were preachers of goodness and love. They weren't threatening anything more than hatred. I hadn't realized that hatred could be so powerful.

It was with these events that I was expected to be a student and to concentrate on math and history. The world was exploding and cities were on fire, but don't forget to do your homework?

Maybe it was a lame excuse, and maybe I was copping out, or dropping out, as some were calling it, but whatever you want to label it, I entered a phase of life where I just didn't care about the things that I was expected to care about. This is how I continued through the remaining weeks of high school, and it is how I began college. Fortunately for me, it would not be the way I would finish college, but that was going take a while, and I have other stories to tell before I get to that one.

—∞—

The summer of 1968 began in earnest on my eighteenth birthday; or, to be more precise, on the Monday after my eighteenth birthday when I had to go to the draft board to register. All of a sudden, the war in Vietnam became too real.

Ironically, I got my draft card on that day, so the phony draft card I had been using could be disposed of by selling to a younger friend for ten bucks. I also got my classification card, which proclaimed to the world that I was 1-A, which meant I was fit to be drafted and summarily deported to points very far east. Despite the fact that this classification would soon be changed to 2-S, college deferment status, when I enrolled at Saint John's, it made me think about the war and those not fortunate enough to go to college. Would it make me a better student? Not likely.

Once I had taken care of this serious business, I devoted the rest of my summer to my new job at P. Lorillard Corporation, where I worked as a mail clerk. This was a tobacco company, and a great place to work. No one cared that it made and sold cigarettes and that they might not be good for people. It was just a great place to work, and I think I learned as much there as I did in college. In fact, I decided to work there part-time while in college.

That first summer was just terrific. The guys I worked with came from all backgrounds and areas of the city. There were black guys from Brownsville, Jewish guys from Great Neck, and another Irish guy from Brooklyn. The bosses were real New Yorkers, too. No one was shy, and nothing was held back whether it had to do with religion, politics, or even race relations. The one topic they all agreed on, however, was the secretaries in the office.

I soon received my education from the guys who broke me in. As I was escorted on our appointed rounds, I was given the lowdown on each secretary: Who was the one you could count on to report you if you were late; who was the one with suspect maternal lineage; and who was hot. The latter, of course, was usually obvious.

The great thing about these guys was that no one cared where you came from or where you were going. Everyone worked hard, and as long as you did too, you were fine.

It was also great to make a few bucks. I remember that first payday taking home one hundred and twelve dollars! I gave my mother a hundred to put in the bank for college, and she let me keep the twelve left over. I got tokens for the next two weeks, and I was left with eight dollars and thought I had hit the big time. I put a few of that away to buy a stereo that I had my eye on. It cost a hundred bucks, so it would not be until the end of the summer before I could get it, but it would be mine.

I was having such a good time working that I really hated to take the weekend off. I just loved talking to the secretaries when I delivered mail, and then just shooting the breeze with the guys. Because I enjoyed being there so much, the summer just flew by, and before I knew it, I was heading to freshman orientation at St. John's.

The best thing about going to college was that Mike and I would be back together in the same school. PJ was going to Fordham, Trent was going to Manhattan College, and Freddie was going to the College of Aeronautics—all located in the area. Since no one of our group was going away to college, we knew we had at least another four years together.

I'll never forget the first thing the students told us when we got to orientation: "They don't take attendance here." Mike and I looked at each other and right away knew that this college thing was going to be just grand. I mean, in high school, every single second of your day was under the watchful gaze of some teacher. Now we could come and go as we pleased. Just beautiful!

Mike and I compared our schedules as we walked around the campus. Unfortunately, since he was a sociology major and I was majoring in history, we didn't have any classes together and rarely even had time off together. Nevertheless, we planned to travel back and forth to college together most of the time.

When orientation was over, I went back to work. I had told them I would be leaving the Friday before Labor Day, but now I had started to think that I really didn't want to leave. I just happened to mention it to my boss, and he went right in to his boss, and they both called me in to talk about it.

I told them that I could work about fifteen hours during the week, but that I could work all day on Saturdays, and they thought that would be great and offered me a part-time job. The best part is that I would be guaranteed a job, next summer, too. Now I was excited!

—ɯ—

1968 promised to be a good year for the Jets, and I knew Michael and his friends would want to go to as many games as possible, so I thought that I should get my own tickets now that I had money. Mike jumped at the suggestion and gave me the money right on the spot.

I was excited that Mike and I had gotten season tickets for the Jets. Unlike my brother Michael, whose seat was in the upper deck on the fifty-yard line, our seats were in the end zone where we would be subject to the cold and fickle winds of Shea Stadium. But we had season tickets, and that's all that mattered.

There were seven home games at five dollars per game so we would each pay thirty-five dollars to see Joe Willie Namath, AKA Broadway Joe, pick apart defenses. I admit thirty-five dollars was a bit steep, but it was worth it in a big way!

Last season Namath had thrown for over four thousand yards, which was more than anyone had ever done. That's why I had high hopes going into the 1968 season. However, the first game of the season was against the Chiefs from Kansas City. The only thing I liked about the Chiefs was what we called the Kansas City huddle.

When we played a game, the Falcons employed this huddle, which I would usually accompany with my weak rendition of "Going to Kansas City." Basically, all the guys stood with their backs to the defense, and I, the quarterback, faced them. This prevented the opposing team from getting a hint as to what our next play would be.

Anyway, our first Jets game was against Kansas City at Kansas City. We never beat this team, and to start our season against them would determine what could be expected for the rest of the year.

It was a nip and tuck game all the way. The Jets had a one-point lead with a little over five minutes to go. I had begun to lose hope, but Broadway Joe came through in a super way.

Namath didn't throw a touchdown, but he ate up the entire five-plus minutes with a great example of offensive ball control. The Jets prevailed, and I felt good about our chances for the rest of the year, which was terrific, but far from perfect. On two occasions, Namath threw five interceptions against the worst teams in the league, Buffalo and Denver. Then, late in the year, the most improbable thing happened, and all at the hands of a little girl in pigtails.

The Jets were playing in Oakland against the hated Raiders. I mean I really hated the Raiders, and the Jets did too, especially their defensive lineman, Ben $#@&!@# Davidson. He actually broke Joe's jaw on one occasion.

Anyway, the Jets were beating the Raiders with only a few minutes to go when a mail boy at NBC decided that they should preempt the Jets and start broadcasting the kids' movie *Heidi*.

This guy wasn't really a mail boy, but he ended up as one after this fiasco. NBC did go back to the game after they realized the stupidity of their error, but by then the Jets were losing. The last thing I saw was the referee marking off a fifteen-yard penalty against the Jets for unsportsmanlike conduct.

But just as the ref was placing the ball on the ground, he threw another flag. The Jets defensive end was barking at the ref, and every time the ref got to the point of putting the ball down, the Jet player must have made another comment that the ref did not like and continued to march off another fifteen yards. The upshot of this is that Heidi and the Raiders beat the Jets.

This game had grave implications for the Jets. Not only was it a critical loss, as we were nearing the end of the season, but it also put Oakland in the lead of the western conference. This meant that there would be a good chance that the Jets would face them if we were lucky enough to go to the championship game.

What actually transpired was a real break for the Jets. The Raiders and Chiefs had to play a playoff game for the conference title because they were tied after the regular season. I really didn't have a favorite in this game, as either opponent would have given the Jets a hard time. The only good news was that the Jets were already in the championship game, and it would be played at Shea.

Oh yeah, Michael, Mike, and I went to the game.

As I alluded to earlier, I am not a great dancer, but I got to dance up a storm on December 29, 1968 at the AFL championship game.

This was another one of those games that you just had to go to. Mike and I had tickets because we had season tickets, but the rest of the guys did not. Nevertheless, we all took off the morning of the game and headed to Shea. Somehow, Trent, PJ, and Freddie were going to get into the game.

Mike and I headed inside, leaving the guys to their own devices, and we would hook up with them after the game.

The game was a killer. You just never knew with the Raiders and their quarterback, Daryle "the Mad Bomber" Lamonica. If I didn't hate the Raiders so much, I would say he was a terrific quarterback and had a great arm.

However, Namath was on fire, and hit Pete Lammons, the tight end, for a touchdown and then followed with the go-ahead touchdown to Don Maynard. But it was the defense that had to come up big, and they sure did.

The Raiders were driving into Jets territory when Lamonica made a crucial error. He threw a short swing pass to Hewritt Dixon, a running back, but he threw it behind him and incomplete. Well, the Jets defense jumped all over the ball, and it was ruled a fumble, not an incomplete pass. Now all that was left was the dancing.

Mike and I were beside ourselves. I don't think we spoke for the last ten minutes of the game until we were counting down the clock. When we got to zero, we went nuts. How great was this? Our first year as season ticket holders and we were going to the Super Bowl!

Well, cheering in our seats was not sufficient for Mr. O. He ran down to the rail and climbed over it. I ran after him, and when he leaped down to the field, about eight or ten feet, I looked down in fear and amazement and he bellowed at me, "C'mon, Jimmy, let's go!"

I went and jumped down after him into the pandemonium that was Shea Stadium. We patted some of the players and each other, and we danced like we had never danced before. It was just amazing.

We stayed as long as we could and just looked around in wonder of it all. We later hooked up with the guys, and Michael and his friends, and we all had a great post-game experience.

We were set to play the Baltimore Colts, who had completely destroyed the Cleveland Browns thirty-four to nothing. But today we celebrated our victory.

—𝔪—

New Year's came and went, and finally the big day arrived: January 12, 1969. The sixties were coming to an end, and in my mind at least, so was the dominance of the National Football League. The Jets would prevail over the dominant Baltimore Colts.

I was one of a very small group of Leland Avenue dwellers who felt certain of that. Of course, Mike and the guys were Jets fans, but not too many other people were. Some didn't like Namath and his white shoes and Fu Manchu mustache and his cocky attitude. When one of the reporters asked him about the game, he said, "We're gonna win; I guarantee it." This was outrageous to all but Jets fans.

That morning I had gone to the ten o'clock Mass as usual, and as I headed home, I ran into one of the local characters of Leland Avenue, Whitey.

"Hey, hey, hey, Jim-m-m-m-my. Whaddya think?"

I replied, "Whitey, we're gonna win. I guarantee it!"

Namath played the most close-to-the-vest game I had ever seen him play. He threw one bomb to Maynard that was caught just on the end line and ruled out of bounds. But it was enough to put the Colts on notice.

From that point on, Namath was able to pick the Colts apart with short, surgical passes to George Sauer, our split end.

The Colts, for their part, self-destructed at every opportunity. Even the great Johnny Unitas threw an interception, though he did finally get the Colts on the scoreboard. By then, however, it was too late, and the Jets won. Namath was the Second Coming in New York.

Perhaps the best part of the day was going to Hoch's later that night to pick up all the newspapers and jab all the Giants and NFL fans. It was a day of days.

CHAPTER 15

THE END OF THE SIXTIES

The rest of the winter was taken up by all-day Monopoly marathons in PJ's basement interspersed with a few football games in the snow. We had a huge snowfall, and I actually missed a few weeks of classes, which was just grand.

You see, college began where high school left off, and if I were to be really honest, I would much rather have been a full-time mail clerk at P. Lorillard. But that minor skirmish over in Vietnam encouraged me to remain in school.

However, even though I was motivated to stay in school, I really wasn't motivated to do well in school. I am a lummox and I know it.

Despite my academic malaise, I had a great sense of history. The year 1969 was of tremendous historical importance.

Of course, the year began with the Jets defeating the NFL Colts in the Super Bowl. Then, on June 8, the Yankees had another Mickey Mantle Day.

This Mickey Mantle Day, unlike the previous one when I was in high school, was held to honor Mickey by retiring his number. Just thinking about that day makes my hands sting. I don't know how long it lasted, but the ovation we gave Mickey seemed to go on and on. I clapped every second of it. No one wanted to stop, but we did when Mickey began to speak.

He started by evoking the immortal words of Lou Gehrig, which every true Yankees fan has heard all his life, "I consider myself to be the luckiest man on the face of this earth."

When I heard him say this, all I could think about was my father, and how he had grown up a Yankees fan watching Babe and Lou, and here I was in the same stadium hearing a baseball player I loved talking about my dad's hero.

Baseball is history, and it is every bit as important as any election or law that gets passed. Baseball has defined us even as it has entertained us.

While I was still enjoying this brush with history, Neal Armstrong stepped out of the lunar module and walked on the moon. My God, we got to the moon just as President Kennedy said we would! Although he never lived to see the day, anyone who remembered his proclamation that we would reach the moon by the end of this decade had to think of him on that day in July of 1969.

I don't know what it was about 1969. Maybe it was because 1968 had been such a disaster with the two assassinations and the riots and all, but 1969 sure had a lot going on.

Another thing that occurred later in the year was the New York Mets won the World Series. They were called the Miracle Mets, and it really was an apt name for them because they came out of nowhere and became the best team in baseball.

Now, I wasn't a Mets fan, and while it killed me that my Yankees were Mickey Mantle-less and in last place, I still had to root for the Mets as a New York team.

Then something truly remarkable happened. The New York Knicks went on a run, and it looked like they were going to have a special year. The basketball and hockey seasons both begin in the middle of fall, so the seasons span two years. The Knicks didn't win anything in 1969, but they were poised to do something really special in 1970.

I mentioned earlier that we used to have Monopoly marathons in PJ's basement. Well, they later included other activities besides just playing Monopoly. Sometimes I think that I spent a year of my life in PJ's basement.

One of the things that we loved doing was listening to the Knicks on radio. Home games were never televised, and the only source of game coverage was the radio. Marv Albert was at the microphone, and if he said, "Yes, and it counts," once, he must have said it a thousand times. We loved it because it meant the Knicks were kicking ass, especially Boston's.

But before the Knicks would weave a trifecta of New York sports fantasia, we had to put the 60s to rest.

One of us had the bright idea of going to Times Square for New Year's Eve. No one we knew had ever done that, and it really did seem like one of those things you had to do at least once in your life. I guess we thought it was like going to Mardi Gras in New Orleans. Anyway, PJ, our friend Louie, and I set out for the Great White Way on December 31, 1969.

The rest of the guys must have had dates or sense. Not sure why we didn't have either, but the three of us set out on the number 6 train for an adventure. Oh, yeah, there was going to be another transit strike at 2:00 a.m.

We prepared for our outing in PJ's basement, and while the temperature was in the low 30s, our internal temperature was warm and cozy. We got down to Times Square early enough to get even cozier. I got so cozy I wanted to give the world the peace sign.

You've seen the big spotlights that they shine in the sky at Hollywood gala events or at used car lots when they have a load of lemons to unload. Well, they had a spotlight right on 42nd Street, and I attempted to insert my hand in its beam to flash the world the peace sign—you know, like Commissioner Gordon sends for Batman. Well, fortunately, PJ intercepted me and I never got the chance to do serious harm to my hand.

The rest of the night was as you might imagine. In fact, it is no use telling you anymore; you might as well just imagine it.

We got to 125th Street at 1:55 a.m. on January 1, 1970, and only had a fifteen-minute wait for the Parkchester local. Unlike back in high school, this time there was no transit strike.

—~—

I worked full-time in the mailroom during our Christmas break, which ended in late January. Going back to school for the spring semester was not exactly something I was looking forward to.

The good news was that I was really busy. Between work and school and getting back and forth to each, I really had to keep myself organized and didn't have time to mess around, which would've been easy to do in those days.

Work actually was a blessing. It became a large part of my social life, at least the part of my social life with women. Not that I actually got involved with anyone, but at least I socialized with them.

School offered little in the way of a social life. Most students at St. John's went to school and rushed home, or like me, they rushed to their after-school jobs. It wasn't easy to chat up a girl while waiting for the Q44A or the number 7 train.

The secretaries at Lorillard, on the other hand, were, pretty much, a captive audience, and I served as a pleasant diversion in their otherwise boring day. Some of them actually looked forward to seeing me.

When it was just the guys huddled around an AM radio in PJ's basement listening to the Knicks, at least I could convince myself that I had women in my life. But listening to the Knicks really was something special that year.

The Knicks were in the playoffs, and they were on a roll. They beat Boston to win the eastern conference, and now they were playing the Lakers in the championship series. Nothing, however, was coming easy, and with our captain on the shelf due to a bad knee injury, we lost game six, and everything was on the line in game seven.

Because game seven was held in Madison Square Garden, it wasn't televised, so we huddled around the radio in PJ's basement one last time. The atmosphere was fantastic. We even made a punch that was more akin to rocket fuel than fruit punch. In addition to assorted juices and liquors, a pint of Bacardi 151 was added for character.

Oddly enough, it tasted pretty damn good—not harsh at all. Nevertheless, we had a hint of exactly how potent the Bacardi was when PJ threw a lit match into the empty bottle. The faint residue lit up like a gas flame at the refineries on the Jersey Turnpike. A whistle accompanied the light show, like that on a steam locomotive. We gained little comfort thinking this was coursing through our digestive tracts.

Now for game seven.

The game seemed to last only about ninety seconds, though it actually started with the pre-game festivities. Competing with the crowd, Marv Albert, the Knicks announcer, yelled that Willis Reed was living up to his role as captain and was walking onto the court and taking practice shots. This was too much. The game was now firmly in the bag. The Garden's faithful were ecstatic, as were all of us in PJ's basement. Let the game begin!

The Knicks won the tip-off and moved the ball into the offensive zone where Captain Willis got the ball and took a turnaround jumper. *Swish!* The Garden was out of control. Then there was an intercepted pass, and Willis Reed once again had the ball.

He took another shot, and the game was over. It had consisted of just four points, a mere two shots. Some might remember that Walt Frazier scored thirty-four points and was really the reason we won, but nobody ever forgot those two shots that Willis made in the opening seconds of the game.

New York had its trifecta. It began with the Jets winning the Super Bowl in January of 1969, continued in October with the Mets winning the World Series, and culminated with the Knicks winning the NBA championship in the spring of 1970. We witnessed a rare era in New York sports. The only thing missing from this group was the Yankees, but they had even started to come back from the dark days after Mickey retired.

Sports only served to distract me from what was going on in Vietnam. When I was in high school, there was a time when I was sure that we had a right to be there and to fight the communists. Now, however, college students all over the country were protesting and burning their draft cards. I never burned my draft card, not because I was such a flag-waving patriot, but because I needed my draft card to get into bars.

In the spring of 1970, something happened that affected the way I viewed the war in Vietnam. Before that, however, I experienced the first of two life-changing events.

It was a typical Friday night. A bunch of the guys met in our usual meeting place, Al's Wines and Liquors, on the corner of St. Lawrence and Westchester Avenues.

It was a unique hangout, and as PJ liked to point out, it allowed us to eliminate the middleman in pursuit of alcohol. We went right to the source. Actually, Freddie worked there, and since the store was securely ensconced in

Plexiglas, it was the safest place in the Bronx. The owner didn't mind us hanging out there because we were a dedicated focus group that sampled the newly arrived craft wines. Our favorite was Bali Hai, and at fifty-five cents a pint, the Nectar of the Gods, as PJ and I called it, was a bargain.

After partaking in our intoxicants, we hopped into a cab and headed over to Fordham where the promise of coed interactions awaited. I was in the spring semester of my sophomore year at St. John's, and PJ was a sophomore at Fordham. Since we lived much closer to Fordham, we always went to the Ramskeller on Friday nights. They had a band and served beer in those lovely plastic cups, and they had coeds, which I may have mentioned already.

Now, you may have heard the expression freshman twenty, which refers to the phenomenon of first-year college students putting on twenty pounds. I invented that. Actually, it was the junior thirty, and it came about in my third year of high school, so by sophomore year in college, I was packing large. This is important to know because of what happened later that night.

We got to the Ramskeller about eight o'clock that night, and it seemed like the usual crowd was there. The band was loud and the beer was cold. PJ and I were sitting at a table by ourselves. The rest of the guys were mingling, I suppose. PJ and I imbibed a little of this and a little of that, and soon it was nearly midnight. PJ and I were feeling little pain by then, but we had slowed down our intake. Then without warning, PJ committed a real niceness.

He looked at me with a big grin and said "Nude, I got a diet for you, and you're gonna do it." Now, not many people possess the right combination of good humor, compassion, and love for a friend to pull that sentence off without devastating the intended beneficiary, but PJ had those qualities. I heard him, and I accepted what he had to say. My life was forever changed that night. That was the first life-altering event that spring.

The second life-altering event occurred a few months later. On May 4, 1970, four students were shot at Kent State University while demonstrating against the war in Vietnam. Because of this event, all the universities throughout the country were shut down. I finished my sophomore year at St. John's, and I was leaving the campus to go to my after-school job at P. Lorillard. I picked up a newspaper, and when I saw the photo on the front page of a girl kneeling over a dead body at Kent State, I was struck with horror. The terror and pain exhibited by that picture went to the core of my being.

I realized that I was not involved in anything. I had no values. I was hardly a college student because I cut class often and rarely did any work at home. I was nowhere.

We all can remember times in our lives when we have made life-changing decisions. I had made one a few months ago regarding my weight, and I was well on my way to changing my life in that regard. Now, I was poised for my intellectual epiphany, and I resolved to succeed in this endeavor as well.

My mother was an avid reader, and she was forever urging me to read. I took her lead, finally, and joined the Book of the Month Club. I figured that if I made a financial investment in books, I was sure to read them. I did read those books and continued to read many more. I was now determined to rescue my college career.

I read about the war and did not like what I read, but I was still a kid from the Bronx who was raised to love America, so I didn't get involved in any anti-war stuff initially. I continued to read and learn, and, also, by the end of the summer of 1970, I had lost fifty pounds. Love, rather than war, was on my mind now.

I had heard from a friend that if you worked for the Nelson Rockefeller re-election campaign for governor of New York, you would get fifty bucks a week. This was big money back in the day. I didn't especially like Rocky, but I loved the fifty dollars. I thought I should pay PJ back for his kindness, and I told him of this great opportunity. So, the two of us headed out one Saturday morning to a Rockefeller rally in Astoria, Queens.

Louis Lefkowitz was the state's attorney general at the time, and he was speaking to the crowd from a platform erected in the street. He was talking like a character in a Cagney or Edward G. Robinson movie.

"Hey, now listen ta dis," he uttered. PJ and I looked at each other and tried to keep from laughing out loud. But we kept ourselves under control and handed out literature and campaign paraphernalia. Our favorites were the Right on Rocky buttons.

Well, we never got the fifty bucks, but I continued to work for the campaign. I handed out leaflets, and the night before the election, I teamed up with a bunch of Right On Rocky supporters and put up posters all over Lower Manhattan. The best part was that I was able to go to the Biltmore Hotel for the election night festivities.

That was a lot of fun, and it was just like you see on TV. Balloons were everywhere, as were rich people dressed to the nines. One of the guys that I had gotten friendly with took me by the arm and ushered me to a private room where they were having a party. It was there that I met Leslie.

Leslie was a blonde bombshell. Her family was from Boston, and they were rich. How rich you ask? They thought the Kennedys were paupers. I couldn't care less about that, as I was only interested in her, not her money. We hit it off and went out the next night to the Electric Circus. This was a laser light show shooting gallery. Zoned-out people stared off into bolts of light and images of paramecia. She liked it. We continued to go out for a few months.

She had a sister and asked me to bring a friend on one of our dates. This is how I paid PJ back.

The night of the big date, PJ and I left our humble abodes on Leland Avenue and headed to the downtown 6 train. When we got to Leslie's school, the girls met us in the parlor. The first thing Leslie's sister said to PJ was, "Why aren't you wearing any socks?"

The night got better, though, and we had a pretty good time. As we were leaving, PJ kissed the sister goodbye, and I attempted to do the same with Leslie. Now, Leslie was not svelte. She wasn't fat, but she wasn't running in any track meets, either. Anyway, I made my move, and she ducked me like I was about to mug her. *Okay, she's shy*, I thought.

Nevertheless, I continued to go out with her. She told her mother about me, which I thought was a good sign. Her mother was concerned about my radical tendencies. She would have loved PJ. He was so put off by the two debutantes that he vowed to join the SDS.

We went on and on, and still there was no kissing. By the way, this was the era of the sexual revolution. Finally, as Christmas vacation loomed, and Leslie would be going home for a month, I put my cards on the table.

I told Leslie that I wanted more out of our relationship. Hell, I wanted a relationship. In the midst of pleading my case, I developed a severe nosebleed. So, there I was snorting blood back up my nose saying, "Leslie, I really think this will work."Then she uttered the most fateful words that I would ever hear: "Jimmy, I think you would be much better off with a nice Irish girl from the Bronx."

Mother of Mercy! From that point on, I hated nice Irish girls from the Bronx—for a few months anyway.

Well, Leslie was weak, and she finally caved in. She said that she would mull it over while on break, but that if she came back committed to have a relationship with me, I damn well better be committed to her, too. I got a little nervous when I heard that. I didn't need to be.

—∞—

The day before Christmas, I headed to work full of the Christmas spirit. I even gave my seat on the subway to an old man. He must have been at least sixty. I think karma was the word I had heard in my Hindu studies class. This promised to be a fun day at work as there was going to be a host of Christmas parties with just a little eggnog and other holiday sprits of the inebriating kind. There is nothing like a little drinking on the job to make the season bright, and maybe a few of the secretaries.

I got to work and found that the boys in the mailroom had already started drinking. The one good thing about working for a tobacco company was that practically everyone smoked, so there was always a good, healthy fog hanging low over the offices. Therefore, picking up the scent of the odd drink or two was next to impossible. Besides, we could never compete in drinking games with the salesmen. Those guys could drink!

The height of the day was the annual Christmas bonus. Unlike last year when we had to lug it home, this year's was sent home by UPS. It wasn't a bag of money, though; it was a box of turkey. They also gave us a carton of Kent that I would pass along to my Uncle James who would sell it to his customers. We were also paid that day even though it wasn't payday, and we were given an extra week's thank-you bonus. I was so surprised that I immediately went out to spend it.

There was a Korvette's on 43rd Street and a Sam Goody's, both of which would help me spend my money while I added to my record collection. Sam

Goody's had a more extensive collection of records, but Korvette's always had a sale. I bought most of my records there—three albums for ten bucks. You couldn't beat that. The one album I wanted to get was *Jesus Christ Superstar*, a rock opera that had just come out. I had heard a few songs from the album on WNEW FM, and they sounded great. Plus, the album was religious, and this was Christmas, wasn't it?

Fortunately, we had a half-day, so I was able to do some other shopping. I got my father a book on the Yankees and my mother a bottle of perfume. I had already gotten everyone else a gift except the guys. We never exchanged gifts unless it came out of the refrigerated wine section of Al's Wine and Liquors. I would shop there later.

It was getting pretty cold, and there was a hint of snow in the air—you could almost smell it. After an early dinner, I headed over to Parkchester and did a little last minute shopping in Macy's. I always liked going shopping on Christmas Eve. It just seemed the Christmassy thing to do. I felt that I hadn't gotten my parents enough, so I shopped for them. I saw a nice pair of leather gloves for my father and a beautiful scarf for my mother. (I was into scarfs.) I even had them gift-wrapped. That was enough to test whatever Christmas spirit I had.

The giftwrapping department was in the basement of Macy's, and as you would expect, it was pretty crowded. I hate waiting in lines. When I was a kid, back in fourth grade, my parents sent me to the bakery for rolls and buns after the ten o'clock Mass. When I came home empty-handed, the family went nuts. "Didn't you go to the bakery?" they all shouted at once. The eggs and bacon were ready, the coffee had been poured, and everyone was waiting for breakfast to be served.

So, when I replied, "Yeah, I went to the bakery, but the line was too long," they looked like a posse that had just caught the bad guy.

I learned my lesson back then, and I stayed in the giftwrapping line no matter what. As I got closer to the desk and the lone woman wrapping gifts, I could tell that she had not yet been haunted by the ghosts of Christmas past, present, or future. She was ranting, raving, and telling no one in particular that she was not going to take it anymore. She had this rich southern drawl, which led me to believe that she would not be a Yankees fan, if you know what I mean. Nevertheless, I stayed in line.

Finally, my perseverance paid off, and I was next in line, but just as I placed my items to be wrapped on her desk, the lady had one final tirade and proclaimed to anyone who could hear, "That's it! I've had enough. Go and wrap your own goddamn presents." Fa la la la la la la la la!

I stopped at Womrath's bookshop, which had wrapping paper on sale, and did my own "goddamn wrapping," as previously instructed.

After depositing my gifts under the tree, I deposited a little splash of Numero Uno, a gift from last year, behind my ear and made haste to Al's Wine and Liquor emporium. Because of the holiday, there would be no purchases of Bali Hai or Strawberry Hill. No, I would splurge and go for the good stuff: Cold Duck. Oh, the boys would be in rare form tonight.

As I was leaving, I ran into PJ and Trent, and they loved the Cold Duck idea and bought a few extra bottles. They were afraid they were coming down with a cold so they wanted to take care to get all the vitamins they could. We headed back to PJ's, and as I was talking about my day, the purchase of *Jesus Christ Superstar* came up. PJ told me to get it and bring it to his house, and to get Mike on the way. PJ and Trent were going to get Freddie. We were going to have one apostolic moment complete with Cold Duck and whatever other intoxicants we could locate.

The five of us made our greetings to PJ's mom and his brother Jim as we made our way up to PJ's attic suite. He had this great poster on the wall that read, *Suppose they gave a war and nobody came?* He also had a strobe candle that was pretty cool to watch, especially as the evening wore on.

Before long, the Cold Duck was uncorked, or rather unscrewed, as in fact were we.

PJ, remembering that I had brought the album, put it on the turntable. Because it was a rock opera, it came with a libretto, and after a bottle or four of Cold Duck, we began to sing along. We were a sight, man, a real sight. Whatever we lacked in musical ability, we made up for with enthusiasm.

This went on for hours. We had to replay a few songs because we just didn't get all the words down pat, and there was only one book for the five of us. Finally, the record was over and Jesus was taken down from the cross. This wasn't exactly the Christmas theme that I wanted to celebrate, so I suggested a little Bing Crosby and the Andrews Sisters. PJ didn't have that, but he did have the Animals singing "Man-Woman," but in a room full of lonely guys, we didn't need that reminder. I looked at the clock, and it was almost midnight. I suggested we go to church.

"What? Are you out of your freaking mind?" they all sang at once. In fact, the harmonic balance they achieved on this one occasion far outshone our entire performance off Jesus Christ Superstar.

I explained why it would be a good thing. I began to sound like one of the Moonies you would see on Forty-Second Street, but I persisted, nonetheless. I hit below the belt with, "Think how happy your mothers would feel if you went to Mass for Christmas," and no one could look me in the eye after that. We had one more sip of Cold Duck and set out for Blessed Sacrament.

Midnight Mass was always a bit of a freak show. It was always mobbed with people in between parties. Not having become totally blasted, they all felt no pain for the most part. We got there about five minutes before Mass and were able to scout out the attendees. We were shouting across aisles and giving peace signs all around us, and while it wasn't exactly Woodstock, it wasn't exactly like Mass on Sundays, either. We were singing "Hark! The Herald Angels Sing," but nobody else was. We were given many looks, but then all of a sudden it caught on, and we had the church singing. I don't think the priests were too happy, but we all settled down once the entrance bell rang and the organ started playing.

We stopped singing all right, but then we started wishing everyone Merry Christmas and hugging and kissing any girl in our immediate grasp. Suddenly, I was back in the good graces of my friends as they all agreed that coming to church was not that bad an idea after all. Then Monsignor Hart gave his sermon.

Here we were, filled with glad tidings, celebrating the birth of our Savior Jesus Christ, and guess what Monsignor Hart decided to sermonize about? The Star of Bethlehem? The Three Wise Men? The Shepherds? Nope! Abortion was the topic of the day.

In his best fire-and-brimstone rant, complete with the appropriate gesticulations and even expectorations (I felt sorry for the people in the first pew, because I think he did spit on a few of them), he brought us right out of first century Bethlehem and into the controversy of all controversies of twentieth-century America.

Mike said, "Merry Christmas to one and all."

Trent said, "God bless us, Jimmy Newell."

But PJ said, "Nude, that's the last freakin' time you ever get me going to church with you."

CHAPTER 16

We All Want To Change The World

Well, our Christmas break came and went, and I anxiously waited to hear what Leslie had decided. I called her, and she repeated her "you need a nice Irish girl from the Bronx" refrain. I was devastated, but life goes on, right?

The following week I got the Sunday papers on Saturday night and headed home. I was going through the "Week in Review" section of the *Times* when my mother came into the kitchen with the *Times Magazine*.

She put the magazine on top of my "Week in Review," and right there on the cover, what did I behold but a beautiful picture of Leslie hard at work in her school library.

"That's her, isn't it?" my mother asked.

"Yeah, that's her."

Ah well, what are you going to do? If God wants to bust your chops, He's gonna do it. Nothing you can do about it.

The spring semester of junior year was a heavy semester for me. I was taking eighteen credits, and every course had a term paper required. It was a good thing I had had my epiphany, or else I never would have survived. In addition to the papers and getting all my research done, I managed to attend a few lectures. The St. John's Peace Committee hosted one of them.

Naturally, the war was the focus of these talks, as it continued to dominate the news, and there was a sense that the tide was turning in Middle America regarding the war. I joined the Peace Committee and eventually another group, the Student Mobilization Committee, an offshoot of the SDS.

My mother approached me with a pile of mail from these groups and wanted to know what was up.

I said, "Mom, I'm revolting!"

She replied, "There, there, Luv, don't let that Boston hussy get you down."

I said, "No, Mom, I mean that I am rebelling! I'm getting involved in the anti-war movement." She may have shaken her head a bit, but I forget.

Well, I handed out leaflets down in Union Square, I wrote letters to Nixon, and I attended meetings at school. One of the activities that the Peace Committee coordinated was the St. John's representation at the big march on Washington scheduled for that April. We were going to get a bus and head down there as a group. The date was April 24, 1971, and we would leave at two o'clock in the morning.

I left 1261 Leland around midnight; I was going to catch the Q44 bus to Flushing and then transfer to the Q28 at Union Turnpike. This would take me about an hour and a half. I got to the campus in plenty of time and met up with a bunch of people. I got talking to this Vincentian priest from St. John's, and we sat together on the bus. Now, this was ironic, because one of my motivations for getting involved in the movement was to meet girls. I was looking for peace in every aspect of the term, and to be sitting next to this Vincentian priest was not going to aid in that quest. But it was a good day, and he was a good guy.

In fact, I was talking to him about the Mass that had been held outside the administration building at St. John's for the four who were killed at Kent State. I told him that it was the most powerful Mass I had ever attended. He thanked me, as he had been the celebrant.

We got to DC and we walked or marched, and we were not alone. Reports had the crowd at three hundred thousand strong. Peter, Paul, and Mary sang "Blowin' in the Wind," and Country Joe did the "Fish Cheer," and we all helped him spell it. I did not see any violence. People were happy and appeared to be earnest, and it made for a magnificent picture in all the Sunday papers. Whether it did any good, I couldn't tell you. It would be another four years before the war officially ended.

We got on the bus and headed back to St. John's. We were all pretty tired, but in good humor. I got home to Leland Avenue around midnight, and when I walked in, my mother was up waiting and said the most shocking thing: "I'm glad you went."

It made me realize that my parents were the children of an America that no longer existed, but they didn't pine for the good old days. They wanted the future to be better. They wanted America to progress, not to go back in time. They had seen the same TV news I had watched. They saw the names of all the dead soldiers scrolling down the screen on Channel 5 every Friday night, and they did not want their sons to be on that list. This wasn't World War II.

They saw how the Kennedys and Martin Luther King were gunned down because of their beliefs, and they had been gunned down in America by Americans. This was not the same country my parents had known all their lives, and someone had to fix that. Maybe my mother thought that was what I was trying to do, and maybe it was.

No sooner had I returned from Washington than I had to really buckle down with schoolwork. I had several twenty- to thirty-page term papers to do that involved much research and trips to various libraries around the city.

One of the papers I was doing involved the history of the American Indian during the New Deal era. This involved frequent trips to the Museum of the American Indian, which had an extensive collection of books, articles, and other written material. I also spent nearly every Saturday afternoon after work in the main branch of the New York City Library. Sometimes after a heavy Friday night soiree, it was more sleeping than researching.

Nevertheless, I got my papers done, but it was not pretty. I had to put in a few all-nighters typing, and I ran out of Wite-Out at one point, so one paper was pretty much a typo mess. After typing until 6:00 a.m., there would be no more rewrites.

I handed the last paper in, and all that was left for me to do to end my junior year was to have my senior year picture taken. My advice to future soon-to-be-seniors is never to schedule your senior picture for the day after an all-nighter. It was not pretty. My hair, which was always unmanageable, had a mind of its own this particular morning. Although I had joined the rest of America and had grown out my hair, my parents were okay with it as long as I kept it clean and somewhat neat. But even their good nature would have been severely tested by the picture that appeared in my yearbook. I hid the yearbook, and no one was ever the wiser.

Summertime was here, and the Fourth of July weekend was looming. We were sitting around PJ's basement, as we continued to do, ruminating over current events, and no one had a date. Not wishing to have the same problem for the Fourth, we outlined our options. PJ wanted to go to the Hamptons.

I had never been east of Jones Beach, and after our debacle last Fourth of July at the Jersey Shore, I wasn't so keen on going. The debacle of which I write is still hard for me to fathom. There were nine of us, and one of the guys had college friends who had a house down in Ship Bottom on Long Beach Island. It sounded like a no-brainer: hot weather, hot girls, and a place to take a shower. It was a no-brainer all right, and we were the ones without the brains.

We drove down on a Friday afternoon, and we got there in relatively good shape. We had to pick up one of the guys who was in on the house, and we should have known something was up. He didn't seem happy to see all of us. No one else noticed this, but I had a bad feeling.

Nevertheless, soon we were on LBI and starting to enjoy our weekend at the Shore. Now, some of our hosts took exception with the methodology we chose to celebrate the beginning of summer, and after a short debate, we were asked to leave the premises. I don't think we lasted an hour before we were kicked out.

We weren't about to give up and drive home; that would come later.

We drove up and down the island looking for motel rooms until we finally found one in Surf City. One room is what we found, and it was a small room. It had a black and white TV and a window for climate control. It had difficulty accommodating a nine-by-twelve piece of cheap linoleum and had but one twin size bed that would be better described as a cot. It also had a hard desk chair. I got lucky. I got the chair to sleep on. We had nine guys in a room that one person would find uncomfortable and distasteful. Nevertheless, we were not there to sleep, but to party, right? Well, no.

The one thing that we neglected to consider after crossing the George Washington Bridge was that we had gone from a state where the legal drinking age was eighteen to one where you needed to be twenty-one to get into a bar. We were reminded of this fact not fifteen minutes after paying for our room and trying to enter one of the nearby bistros. Now what?

We patrolled the beach into the evening hoping to find people who were having a party and needed more revelers. As you might imagine, we were not successful. We found an ice cream stand that was tended to by a rather attractive girl, so we lined up for some ice cream. I am not sure where she was from, but she had a southern drawl that made you think of Scarlett O'Hara. I thought I would charm her with my wit.

"Y'all from the south?" I asked, "Well, I'm from the south,". "South Bronx, that is."

The boys thought that was pretty funny, but our Belle didn't find much humor in it, so we took our ice cream and went back to our room and watched *Forbidden Planet* on our black and white TV.

The next morning we piled into the car and headed back to the Bronx.

Some of the guys thought about trying out the Hamptons, but we figured it was too late to do anything. PJ vowed that the same thing would not happen on Labor Day weekend.

It was that Labor Day last year that set the stage for this year's Fourth of July. PJ and a couple of guys finally made it out to the Hamptons, and PJ came back as an evangelist of east-end living. He had been to the Promised Land known as Hot Dog Beach. From that moment on, he was planning our trip to the Hamptons for the Fourth of July. Now it was time to realize his vision.

This time we had six guys in Trent's '65 Chevy. In addition to PJ, Mike, Freddie, Trent, and me, Andy was with us. I won't go into much about Andy. Suffice it to say that Andy was responsible for ingratiating himself to most of Hot Dog Beach by offering much of the supplies we had rationed for the weekend.

We headed out on Friday night and arrived at Hot Dog Beach around ten. The place was mobbed. There was a band playing, and there was much frivolity in the air. We really were in the Promised Land, and we acknowledged PJ as our Moses.

While many of my memories of this night have been washed away with the surf and good cheer that we enjoyed, others are better left for private recollection when the boys get together in the future. But one event should be written down for posterity. It involved a character by the name of John Tent Man.

John Tent Man was this guy whom PJ met on last year's Labor Day trip, and he was afforded mythological stature. For one thing, he had a tent. He also wore an eye patch, which I guess made him look like a pirate. For this or whatever reason, PJ sought out John Tent Man everywhere we went on Hot Dog Beach.

It was getting so late that it was almost early morning. The stars were like nothing I had ever seen outside the Museum of Natural History. It was intoxicating to look up at them. But soon the stars were fading and the dawn was breaking, and we had not yet slept. You see, we were just as prepared for this trip as for last year's, and we had not really thought of a place to stay. PJ and I got separated from the rest of our group, and as we strolled down the dunes, we saw some guys pitching a big tent.

"Come on, Bear," PJ exhorted. Apparently, we had found John Tent Man and company.

Following PJ's lead, we soon found ourselves immersed in a rather sizable tent. We immediately made ourselves at home and set in for a much-needed nap. Unfortunately, our hosts had yet to complete the task of erecting the tent. No matter, we were comfortable and did not mind that they needed to continue working. Soon they were done, and one of our benefactors opened the flap and seemed nonplussed to see us.

"Who the hell are you?" he demanded of PJ, to which PJ replied, "I'm a friend of John Tent Man; you know, the guy who wears an eye patch. I think he's from Staten Island. We were here with him last Labor Day, and we had a great time. My name is PJ, and did I mention I was here last year with John Tent Man, the guy with the eye patch, and we had a really good time?"

Seemingly not satisfied with PJ's rambling explanation about this guy John Tent Man, our host quickly turned to me and asked, "Well, who the fuck are you?"

To which I rather nimbly retorted while pointing at PJ, "I'm a friend of his."

We were soon disinvited from the tent.

You might think that this experience would have put a damper on the rest of our weekend. It did not. The rest of the weekend consisted of memorable events that we were unable to recall in their totality.

What I do recall, however, will be with me forever: sleeping on the beach under the canopy of the Milky Way; eating bologna sandwiches by the Indian Grave by the side of the Long Island Railroad track; using the bathroom at the Hampton Bays Diner to refresh; getting a three-day sunburn/tan that lasted the rest of the summer. These were some of our treasured Hamptons memories.

We got back to the Bronx on Monday afternoon, and we were quite the sight. Not bathing for three days and sleeping on sand will do that to you, I guess. But after a thorough sterilization, several glasses of New York City's finest tap water, and a catnap, we all met together again in PJ's basement, reliving our East End adventure. It was agreed that a good time was had by all.

—⁓—

The end of the summer was quickly approaching. On the first Friday of August, Manhattan College was having one of their Manhappenings. Manhattan College was rated the number one drinking school in the country by *Playboy* magazine, and if you couldn't believe *Playboy*, whom could you believe? Like the rest of us, Trent was about to enter his senior year at Manhattan, and we all piled into a cab to help usher in our last year of college.

We knew a few of the guys up at Manhattan, and we always had a good time at the Manhappenings. They sold beer in cans, not watered down sludge like other places, and they only charged a quarter for the privilege of drinking Schaeffer or Rheingold. And it was cold, quite unlike the Pathmark Beer that PJ and I drank the week before.

It was at the Manhappening that the events of September 3 had their roots—red roots to be precise.

You will remember my ill-fated romance with Leslie, the Bostonian wench who condemned me to a life of falling in love with nice Irish girls from the Bronx. Well, because of her and her prediction, I did all I could do to avoid nice Irish girls from the Bronx. Oddly enough, Trent, of Sicilian heritage, didn't, and was dating a lovely Irish beauty that I would have willingly reneged on my oath for had she not been my friend's girl. I found out too late that the girl I thought he was dating was more of a buddy than a love interest. It was with this in mind that I happened across a stunning redhead standing with a few people we knew.

I asked her to dance, and we hit it off. She found me funny and interesting, so I thought I was home free. "The trouble is," she said, "my father would never approve of you." Those are never good words to hear any female utter.

I didn't want to say that I wasn't particularly interested in making out with her father or that we weren't getting married or looking for a house or anything, so I took the high road. "Why wouldn't he?" I inquired. She then went on to list the ways he would hate me; it may have been in iambic pentameter.

The crux of my problem, it seemed, was my hair and my politics. Here I was again making a case for my worthiness as a suitor just as I had with Leslie six months earlier. I was just as successful this time too. I began to think that my idea of going to law school would be useless. I could never win a case; no jury would ever listen to me.

We said our goodbyes, and I got over it. "A pox on you," I uttered as she walked out the door.

Then before I knew it, Labor Day weekend had arrived. That Friday would be my last day working in the mailroom at P. Lorillard Corporation, and it was the last job I would absolutely love, at least for some time.

As was our custom on paydays, the mail crew went out to lunch at The Blarney Stone, which had the best roast beef sandwiches and coldest tap beer. We had a full hour for lunch on paydays, and we enjoyed every minute of it. We even stretched it an extra fifteen minutes because it was my last day. We topped off our lunch with Tiparillos, as we usually did, and eventually made our way back to the mailroom.

I might have suggested that we go out after work, but it happened to be my mother's birthday, and there was no way I was going to miss Lizzie's birthday. She was sixty-four, and I had my *Sgt. Pepper's Lonely Hearts Club Band* album cued to play "When I'm Sixty-Four" when I got home. I also had a new FM kitchen radio for her, as she had worn out the old Zenith after years and years of daily listening.

Pop and I sang "Happy Birthday," and since the rest of the family would be coming over the next evening, I was able to go out with my friends without feeling too guilty. For some reason, my parents didn't seem too upset that I was leaving.

I made my way down Westchester Avenue heading to our hangout, Al's Wine and Liquors on the corner of St. Lawrence Avenue. Al's offered the unique opportunity to combine work with pleasure. Although we were not officially on the clock like Freddie was, since he actually worked there, we liked to consider ourselves part of Al's R&D division. Our task was to identify the next fad in cheap wines.

As I entered the outer part of the store, I could tell that we had a quorum, and testing had already begun. Not wishing to be left behind, I quickly had Freddie buzz me into the inner sanctum.

You see, Al's had been subjected to one too many hoodlum looking for a quick score, so Al had the entire store ensconced in Plexiglas. Customers could peer through the bulletproof barrier, select their drink for the evening, and have it provided to them through the ingenious air-lock apparatus, thereby providing the clerk with optimum security. It was the safest place for our evening activities.

Just as we were beginning to feel the warmth of our merrymaking, who should walk through the door but Monsignor Hart. You never saw so many guys duck for cover.

"It's Monsignor!"

There we were in our twenties still petrified of the man, as though he could have us kicked out of school for drinking. We survived that scare and proceeded to the task at hand.

The products of our testing procedures this evening included Gallo Pineapple wine, a favorite of Freddie's, Boone's Farm Grape, of which Trent was a devotee, and, of course, the piece de resistance, Bali Hai—the Nectar of the Gods.

At fifty-five cents a pint, Bali Hai offered superior taste at a reasonable price. You didn't need a corkscrew, either, which added to its pint-sized convenience. You had to be careful, though. When you first opened a bottle, you didn't want to get too close as you might singe your nose hair a tad. But once you let it breathe, it was sheer heaven.

I liked to have a Ballantine Beer chaser. How about that? For those of you who are too young to appreciate the significance of my inserting "How about that" into the narrative, Ballantine Beer had been the longtime sponsor for the Yankees on Channel 11, and Mel Allen was the announcer. It was rumored that Mel liked a Ballantine or two, especially during doubleheaders, and "How about that" was his signature call.

I had gotten to the liquor store a little later than usual, and rather than bore you with the other exploits that continued into the far reaches of the storeroom in the back, I will only say that we were soon prepared for a night out on the town. But where to go in the Bronx?

None of the local colleges had anything going on because school would not start until Tuesday, so it was a choice of which local bars we would frequent. PJ always liked going to the Hollow Leg up on Tremont Avenue, but I still had grim memories of the place when it was called the Bronx Irish Center or BIC. I had no desire to rekindle those memories, so I suggested the Castle Keep.

Fortunately, this was a mistake that I wouldn't live to regret.

CHAPTER 17

SEPTEMBER 3, 1971

The Castle Keep was also on Tremont, but down on the corner of Bruckner Boulevard. When we entered, we noticed that no one was there. We increased the attendance by a factor of infinity if you exclude the barkeeps. Not wishing to admit my mistake, I observed that we were probably a little early and that within a half hour we would be up to our eyeballs in pretty coeds. Well, an hour later, there was not a coed, pretty or otherwise, to be found, so we opted to extract ourselves posthaste.

Having taken responsibility for a disastrous decision, I had no alternative than to agree to anything, and PJ chose the Hollow Leg.

Well, I had to admit that he was right, and I was wrong. The joint was jumpin', and they had a band; it had all the makings of a great night. In fact, it was great right away, but not for me. Within a matter of seconds, it seemed, Mike, Trent, PJ, and Freddie were all paired up with good-looking girls, and I was left doing the rope-a-dope, bobbing and weaving all by myself.

I got myself a beer and just looked around. All of a sudden, I made eye contact with the redhead from Manhattan College, but there was something wrong. She was smiling and giving me a come-hither type of look. I was far away from her at the time, and it was a dimly lit bar, after all, so maybe I was misinterpreting signals.

She kept smiling, so I thought *what the heck*. I took a few steps over to where she was seated at the bar, and immediately saw my error. It was not the Manhattan redhead. This was a new, prettier, happy-to-see-me redhead. I had to think quickly, as I was almost right by her side. What would I say?

I said, "I've been admiring you all night." Well, I thought she was going to fall off her barstool she laughed so hard. "That's what you came up with, huh?"

I was dumbfounded, but not by her reply, though she was pretty funny. I was looking at the most beautiful girl I had ever seen. She had long, shoulder-length red hair that flowed down her back. She had the biggest and bluest eyes I had ever seen, but I had seen those eyes before! For the life of me, I couldn't remember where but you don't forget eyes like hers.

I really don't remember what I said next, but I did buy her a rum and Coke, and we talked and talked. Finally, I asked her what her name was, and she said, "Eileen."

She told me she was a senior in high school. I thought, *Oh, my!*

She told me she was seventeen. I thought, *Oh, God!*

Then she told me that she was Kevin and Jimmy Rooney's sister, and I thought, *OH, SHIT!*

You never wanted to go out with the little sister of two brothers, especially when you were twenty-one and she was seventeen. But did I mention those eyes?

She never stopped smiling, and I never stopped talking, which I know most of you won't believe. Before I knew it, we were talking about going home, as it was nearly one in the morning. She hopped off the bar stool, and I almost passed out. She was dragging her left leg! She was a gimp!

What was I going to do? I had to see it through. She still had those eyes. Did I mention her eyes?

Well, I must have looked a sight when I saw her walk because she was really laughing now, uncontrollably.

I asked her, "What's so funny?"

"You are, you big lummox. I had a patellectomy last month—a knee operation."

"Oh, the limp, you mean," I said.

"Yeah, Einstein, the limp. A little exercise and I should be good as new."

"Oh, so you need exercise, huh? How about I exercise you all over Central Park tomorrow?"

She said, "I'd love that!"

Then we stopped talking, and I found myself kissing my new seventeen-year-old girlfriend right there on Tremont Avenue.

I had another idea. "Let's take a bus to the Square and then change for the 42 back to White Plains Road."

"Ok, Sport," she replied. "No sense blowing two bucks on a cab."

"No, no, no, that's not it at all. I just want this night to last as long as humanly possible. I want a nice story to tell our kids."

Then I swear to God she kissed *me*, and there was no way she was seventeen, let me tell you.

At that very moment, I realized I was in love with a nice Irish girl from the Bronx, and that seemed pretty damn good to me.

We took our buses home, and we walked down White Plains Road, but not all the way to her house. Eileen wanted to talk some more. We did a lot of talking right on the corner leaning on the trunk of a Ford Galaxy that was parked on a slanted driveway going down to the garage.

Fortunately, no one could hear us talking, and more importantly, no one could see that we really weren't doing much talking.

I know love at first sight is a romantic notion that no one really buys anymore, but Eileen did, and so did I. It would only take another day or two before we told each other that this was it. We were in it for keeps. But on this night, September 3, 1971, I walked her home and kissed her just once more to get me home. It was both joyful and painful at the same time knowing that it would be only a few hours before I would be picking her up for our first date. I didn't know how I could possibly fall asleep.

I did sleep and got up early, and my mother knew there was someone new in my life.

"So, did you meet someone?"

"Yeah, I did. This is the one, Mom, so you don't have to worry anymore."

"Thanks be to God and Saint Anne! Do you mean I can stop the Novenas?"

"Well, for this, I guess, but there are other things I am sure you will be praying for."

I had only been waiting on the corner of Gleason and White Plains for a few minutes when I saw Eileen hobbling up the block. We both laughed, and she didn't seem disappointed to see me. We walked over to the Oval in Parkchester to take the express bus down to the Park. "Wow, big spender, I was expecting a subway ride today," she teased.

So, this is the way it was going to be: laughter and kissing. That sounded pretty good to me. But I got even for being the butt of the laughter.

We went down to the park and I showed her all my favorite spots including where the statues of the writers are and the folk groups that provided free entertainment. "Don't even think it," I said when she was all set to make a comment about the "free" aspect of the entertainment.

I got even with her twice, and here's how.

I asked her if she wanted to sit on the grass and listen to the music. I then asked her if she wanted lunch. She said yes.

I said, "Good, we'll split a hot dog and an orange soda." Then we did just that, and she admitted, "You got me."

"Not done yet," I replied. I got up as if to put our trash in the receptacle, but I kept walking. Then she really got me.

She yelled out at the top of her lungs that I was abandoning a handicapped girl. There were the looks and then the accusations from the nearby crowd, but then the kissing right in front of the same nearby crowd.

We then started to walk around the park and onto Fifth Avenue. I had my camera with me, and I had been taking a few pictures of her during our jaunt, but I wanted to get one with both of us in it. As we were passing the Sherry Netherland Hotel on Fifth Avenue, I had an idea.

There was a mirror in the lower portion of their front window, so Eileen and I scrunched down and looked into the mirror, and I took a picture of the two of us. It's my favorite picture of Eileen because she looks so happy to be standing next to me.

Our next date was on Labor Day. We went down to Battery Park, and as we were walking along the path among a group of pigeons, I ducked down as though they were going to swoop down on us. Eileen, following my lead, did the same, and when she realized I was only pulling her leg (not the bad one), we both laughed.

A few minutes later, back on the subway, as we were sitting next to each other in comfortable silence, we both looked at each other and, as if we were synchronized at the hip, we simultaneously ducked.

At that moment, I told her I loved her. The next step was to meet the family.

—∾—

The rest of the week was just as amazing. Eileen and I met every day after school to get our homework done or to walk to Macy's or Korvette's. The weekend was fast approaching, though, and so was the ultimate test of our new relationship: I had to meet her mother.

Now, I wasn't stupid, and I knew that any mother would worry about her seventeen-year-old daughter dating a twenty-one-year-old man. I mean, I was still in school, and I really didn't feel that much older than Eileen, but I could understand the concern. Anyway, I would meet Eileen's mom Saturday night after the six o'clock Mass.

Now, I had picked up Eileen at her house on White Plains Road, and her mother had seen me and I had also met her sister, but I never really was introduced or had any conversation with her mother. So, we went to Mass, and I couldn't tell you who said it or what I did or anything. I was preoccupied. But eventually zero hour arrived, and I was walking up the steps to Eileen's house and going through the doorway.

They had a dog, Whimpie, who really saved the day. He was my much-needed icebreaker, and more attention was paid to him when I first came in than to me. When Eileen's mom greeted me, she was very friendly, and for some reason I could hear her Irish brogue even though I could never hear my mother's.

I will never forget the first words Mrs. Rooney said to me:

"Now, Jimmy, would you like a nice, cold soda?"

"Yes, Mrs. Rooney, that would be great," I replied.

"Well then," she said, "you'll be having to go down the corner and get it, and while you're there, could you get me a pack of Kent?"

I went down the corner and got my soda and Mrs. Rooney her pack of Kent.

When I got back from the bodega down the corner, Eileen escorted me into the kitchen for a nice dinner of lamb chops. I had brought Mrs. Rooney a box of candy, and when I told her that I used to work for the company that made Kent cigarettes and I could still get her a carton for free, I was in like Flynn.

We then talked about Sligo and my mother coming from there, and I tried to sound more Irish than I was. We had a good night. At least, I think it was a good night. Who knows if I made a good impression or not?

It was hard enough to get on the good side of a girl, and now I had to worry about an entire family! The next week would provide the opportunity for me to seal the deal, but it would cost Eileen a lot of pain.

On Tuesday, Eileen had a dentist appointment with some sadist on the Concourse. I volunteered to take her because I thought that was what boyfriends did. Her mother looked greatly relieved when she knew I was going to go with Eileen, but I really didn't know why until Tuesday.

The Rooney dentist was this quack that I'll call Dr. De Cruel. I swear I think that was his name. Anyway, Eileen had to have a wisdom tooth pulled, and I figured I'd be there to get her home since she would probably still be under the influence of the noxious oxide or whatever he was going to give her. But that was not the case.

I was in the waiting room listening to terrible music, but it would be only a few minutes before I was hoping he would turn it up louder. Eileen screamed like she was being mugged by a group of Hell's Angels. I had never heard such screaming before in my life. I was pacing and walking in circles with worry—I was a mess. I almost wanted to go into the dentist's office and drag her out of there. Over all of Eileen's screaming, I could hear him say, "Just stop it and let me finish." Great bedside manner this son of a bitch had. Later, when I asked Eileen why the laughing gas or Novocain hadn't worked, she said that he hadn't given her anything. Now I really wanted to clobber the bastard. Anyway, she survived, and so did I.

I drove her home in my VW Beetle and got her settled down. When her mother came home, I could tell that she was grateful that I had been there for Eileen.

—ɯ—

Senior year was starting off great. In addition to meeting Eileen and knowing that she was the one, I was more into my schoolwork than ever before. Although I had started my academic transformation the year before, it was only now that I felt I was getting somewhere. I really regretted all the time and opportunities I had wasted in my first two years of college, but I guess it was better late than never.

The great thing about senior year was that Mike and I were finally able to take the same courses. This was the first time we had been in the same classes ever. Even back at Blessed Sacrament, we had been in different classes, and now in our last year at Saint John's we were finally able to share our intellectual pursuits.

Of course, that did include a number of activities that were not part of the Saint John's curriculum.

Don't make any mistake; we both worked our butts off because we had higher academic aspirations. I had always thought about going to law school, and Mike was thinking about going into social work. He even had me taking some of his sociology classes. We hit the books hard to make sure that senior year would put us in a good position to move up the academic ladder.

I still had a few history courses to take, and one of them greatly affected my future. The course was a colloquia, which meant that it was not your standard lecture and note-taking marathon. We read a book each week and shared ideas, and our professor was especially interested in letting us run the class. It was this class made me think about choosing teaching as a career. It was also the reason that I would opt to get a graduate degree in history instead of going to law school, but first things first.

Back to senior year and our extracurricular activities. That year Saint John's finally built a real student center. It had ping-pong tables, foosball tables, and pool tables. It even had a bar! So when we were not in class or the library, you could bet your bottom dollar that we were sipping a little brew while playing a little eight ball. We weren't frat boys or anything, but we really enjoyed our last year as college students.

Notwithstanding our love of our new college experience, Mike and I set off for the Bronx right after our last class. Life was truly grand. I had it all. I was taking classes that kept me academically stimulated. I was able to enjoy a little of the college experience that I never really had in my first three years. More importantly, I had a girl I loved.

Eileen and I saw each other every day after school. I had gotten over the fact that she was only a senior in high school while I was a senior in college. I think her family was finally getting over it, too.

The one thing I didn't think about when we first started going out was that she would have a whole slew of friends that I would have to meet. I wasn't looking forward to that, but I had to go through the motions to keep Eileen happy.

Eileen kept going on about her best friend Pat and her boyfriend Paul. I was first introduced to Pat one day while ringing the bell at Eileen's house. While waiting, this girl wearing a Saint Helena's uniform, complete with the stupid hat they made girls wear, came bouncing down the staircase in Eileen's house. She was all bubbly and friendly, and then she told me that she was Eileen's sister. I don't think I visibly shook my head when she said this, but I was filled with an immediate sense of dread. What next?

Well, the next was told to me that night. We would be meeting Pat and Paul at the six o'clock Mass at Blessed Sacrament on Saturday. I didn't know what to expect, but I was trying to put on a good show for Eileen. I didn't want to reveal my inner crank face just yet.

Father Rafferty said the Mass, and while we didn't sit with Pat and Paul during the Mass, we met in the vestibule of the church. I was nice, but I was worried all the same.

As you might imagine, Pat and Paul were the same age as Eileen, which meant that I was four years older than everyone in the group. I don't know if it was because the three of them were mature for their age or whether I was really a teenager at heart, but after about thirty seconds of hi how are ya, we were fast friends. Laughter does that to you, I guess. I found that I could not be in Pat's presence without laughing every thirty seconds. She was very appreciative of my sense of humor, as was Paul.

I got the feeling that I was a big hit, and I don't think it was only because I could get them liquor and beer.

After Mass, we went to Eileen's house for dinner. I noticed something right away as we entered the house. We were going to eat in the dining room. This was a momentous event. I only wish I had some kind of a device that I could have used to record this for posterity. I was playing the dining room after only a short stint in the kitchen. I felt like Sinatra finally making the big room in Vegas.

Now that dinner was over, we went into the living room to chat. Well, to be honest we weren't really chatting. We were plotting. The plan was that Paul and I would go out for some soda. When we said the word soda, the girls gave an expressive nod of the head and just enough enunciation to support the conclusion that we had better not come back with soda.

Once outside, Paul and I put the plan into action. First, we would go to the liquor store to get the girls a bottle of wine. Then we would go to the local bodega and get some beer. Paul suggested a foreign beer in lieu of the standard Ballantine. We got a few Heinekens and even a few dark Heinekens. To me it didn't matter, as I had never had anything that wasn't made in New York.

After having made our purchases, we went to the back of the house to enter through the basement door. Of course, the door was locked, and, of course, we couldn't knock. I found myself once again wishing for the Dick Tracy two-way radio that PJ and I had always wanted. We had no way to signal to the girls that we were back and needed them to open the door.

Thank God for Whimpie. If Eileen had not had a dog, I am quite sure Paul and I would still be outside that basement door. I am quite willing to believe, however, that the beer would have been gone despite the fact that we did not have a bottle opener. I got the sense from Paul that he was creative enough to come up with an alternate bottle-opening device.

When Whimpie sensed our presence and made a few barks, the girls realized we were home. They went down to the basement where we would be listening to records and having our potables, and no one would be any the wiser.

I said to Eileen, "I hope our kids won't be sneaking beer into our basement."

"Our kids?" she asked.

"Why, yeah, of course our kids!"

"Ok, I just wanted to make sure."

We then started dancing (I told you it's not all going to be factual), and at that moment, I realized that some monumental things had occurred this night. Not only had I met the couple that would be our best friends for life, but Eileen and I had determined that we would be our best friends for life, too.

CHAPTER 18

LOVE GROWS IN THE BRONX

I found that love relationships take on a whole life of their own. I started going shopping for things I never had shopped for before. I found myself holding Eileen's coat while she was trying pants on in Macy's. I was answering questions about which color sweater looked better and whether beige should be her color that year. I was constantly worrying that I would say the wrong thing. I even started helping with the dusting and vacuuming so that Eileen would have more time on the weekend to go out. But I guess the most significant thing I learned was that all I wanted was to be with Eileen all the time. It didn't matter if we went out or not. Just watching TV on a Saturday night was a treat.

Of course, this meant that my time with the guys became limited, but they were all in the same situation, too, so no one really cared. We still got together to play football on Sundays, and Mike and I still went to Jets games. But the days of going to Al's Wine and Liquors were coming to an end.

I learned that once you're hooked up with a girl, you really change the way you live. It wasn't just me. I saw the same thing happen to all the guys. Once we had settled down with one girl, there was a complete change in how we interacted. The girls took over, and we rarely got together as a group.

It was almost like they realized that if they let us all continue to hang out together, we would never grow up. I can't say they were wrong.

Don't get me wrong, we did socialize from time to time, but never like we did before we settled down with one special girl. There would be no going to the Hamptons and looking for John Tent Man or going to Al's Wine and Liquors looking for the newest cheap wine.

And to be honest, I think it was the guys and not the girls who were happy to put those days behind us. None of us wanted any of our old stories to be told to our new girlfriends. I guess we were pretty smart when you think about it.

The truth is, though, we all were happy with our new loves, and there was no reason to rock the boat, if you know what I mean.

That is why on any given Saturday night, when I used to be sorting out which club to go to, I now sorted out which TV show to watch with Eileen and her mother. That is, of course, on those Saturday nights when Eileen's mom was not hosting the local chapter of the Sons and Daughters or Armagh Soiree.

As I mentioned earlier, my mother came from County Sligo while my father was born in New York City, the son of Arthur Newell of Manchester, England. Now my grandfather, Arthur Newell, while born in Manchester, England, was the son of Michael Newell of County Mayo and Ann Fairhurst of Manchester. I am not sure if they were married in Mayo before they moved to Manchester, where Arthur was born. In any event, they brought Arthur to this country, where he would one day find himself fighting for the United States in the Spanish-American War. He was an excellent marksman, and he competed in a number of sharp shooting events where he won numerous medals.

He was rewarded for his patriotism by being fired for signing a petition to form a union when he worked for a gas company that would one day be known as Con Edison. Ironically, his son, my father, made a career at the same company.

My mother's parents actually came to this country in the nineteenth century, and my grandfather worked on the construction of the Brooklyn Bridge. They eventually went back to Sligo where their children were born.

Now, despite the international roots of my family tree, I never really took note of our heritage. Of course, I did celebrate Saint Patrick's Day, and my mother and I would bake Irish soda bread on a cold winter's day, but aside from these tips of the cap to our Irish background, I never really paid it much attention. Then Eileen and I started going out.

From the moment I brought Eileen home to meet the folks, she was granted royal status. Red hair, blue eyes, and a name like Eileen Rooney made her an instant hit with my mother. My father didn't stand a chance either. Naturally, I was delighted that they took such a liking to her, but the fact that her word was now gospel and mine was given short shrift really annoyed me. But Eileen's family treated me pretty well, so it all balanced out.

Getting back to Eileen's mother's soirees, on a frigid Saturday night in January of 1972, I attended my first Rooney party. These parties were unlike any I had ever attended. For one thing, the age discrepancy of the attendees was the largest of any gathering I had ever attended.

Pat, Paul, and Eileen were all seventeen, and they were the youngest. Then there were those of us in our twenties. Eileen's brothers and sister ranged in ages that I will not record, as I do not wish to piss anybody off. Let's just say they were older than Pat, Paul, and Eileen.

Then there were my parents, Eileen's mom, her friends, and some who were older, and the remarkable thing was that everyone had a great time. Who would have thought that you could have that much fun at a party with your parents? There was much laughing, lots of eating, and just the right amount of drinking. But most importantly, there was music.

There was a trio of Irish musicians that consisted of a fiddler, a piper, and someone on the squeezebox. They had the joint jumping, but it wasn't really hopping until a lass from the good County Armagh gave her roaring rendition of Frankie and Johnny. Man, she was amazing! Eileen's living room was rocking.

Being that it was a Saturday night, and the attendees all had to get up for Sunday Mass, the party came to an end at around two in the morning. However, no one went home until everyone in the house stood up and sang "God Bless America." While many in the house were born across the sea, none took their American freedom for granted. They loved Ireland, but they were Americans.

—⁂—

The rest of the year was one amazing day after another. I don't think Eileen and I went more than two or three days without seeing each other, and that was only because of family visits or school trips.

Now that I was in my senior year, I had to start thinking about what I was going to do next.

I thought it was ironic that no sooner had I gotten the message about what it meant to be a student, than I would soon no longer be a student. I was really struggling with the fact that an adult world waited out there, and I still wanted to be a schoolboy.

Eileen, on the other hand, was on the verge of choosing her career. Even though she was four years younger than I, she was much more focused on what she wanted to do with her life than I ever had been or would be. She knew before she was a senior in high school that she would go to nursing school, and that was that. There was no other choice as far as she was concerned. It turned out that Pat had decided the same thing.

I, on the other hand, didn't have a clue as to what I wanted to do when I graduated. But I eventually had an idea.

I really liked my courses in history and had a couple of professors that I found especially interesting. I decided to continue my study of history by pursuing a master's degree. I just couldn't walk away from school when I had finally started to be a student.

But before I had to worry about a job or a career, there was Eileen's prom and both of our graduations to keep me occupied. The good times continued to roll. We thought about taking a trip to the Hamptons with Pat and Paul before the girls headed off to Saint Vincent's.

Eventually the time came when Eileen had to set off for school, and she planned to live on campus, but she wound up being just a few blocks from where I wound up working while I went to grad school.

As it seemed to be our fate, Mike and I were back together again, but this time we were working together rather than going to school together. Although there were times that you might have thought we were back at Saint John's living as wild college boys, we worked for the City of New York. In fact, Mike got me the job, and he was working on his master's too, so we really didn't have that much time to get into trouble.

It was a good thing that I went to grad school, because between going to class two nights a week and getting all my reading done on the other nights, I hardly had time to be depressed when Eileen was not at home. I still got depressed, though, and I felt that I just couldn't get through the week fast enough.

Once Friday came, I was a new man. It didn't even matter if all we did was stay home and watch TV.

We did manage to go out every now and then with Pat and Paul. We liked going to Flanagan's, the one on the east side. Oh boy, did we have fun there. I wish I could remember.

With both of us kept busy by school, the time just flew by despite the fact that we missed each other during the week.

I think I had really started to fit in with Eileen's family by this time. They realized I was a decent enough guy, and her mom even talked about me going with them on their next trip to Ireland.

Eileen had been there the year before we met, and she had never stopped talking about it. I really started to think seriously about it, knowing that my mother would be happy for me to see the house where she grew up. When Eileen and I started to make our plans, I brought up the subject to my mother, hoping she would come with us, but she would have none of it.

She reasoned that it had been nearly fifty years since she left home to settle in this country, and that it would be much too emotional for her to return. I could understand that.

By the spring of 1974, I had gotten my passport, paid for my airfare, and gotten some sporty luggage. I also managed to buy some clothes that Eileen helped me pick out so that I would not drive her crazy wearing the same powder blue bellbottoms that I had been wearing the last two years.

We were going to be a sizable group heading off to the Emerald Isle. In addition to Eileen and me, her mother, aunt, and cousin would be flying over with us. I was the only man in our group, and I was just a wee bit worried about that, let me tell you. That wasn't the only thing I was worried about. I had never flown in an airplane before. I chose a transoceanic flight as my first time in a plane. I tried not to think too much about that.

During this time of my life, I was an avid photographer. I first got a 35mm camera to take pictures of Joe Namath from our seats in the end zone. So, of course, I would be taking all my camera gear with me on my Irish vacation.

Finally, the big day came.

Before I left for the airport with Eileen's family, I had to go over to see Uncle James and have a talk and a drink. He was as excited about my going to Ireland as I was. The first thing he asked me about was where I intended to travel while in Ireland. To be honest I hadn't given it much thought. I knew I would go up to Sligo to see my mom's hometown and the house where she was born, but outside of that, I didn't have a plan. But Uncle James did.

I said, "I'll probably spend a lot of time in Dublin."

Uncle James replied, "Okay, go to Dublin for a day, but no more. Get out to the country to see the people. That's what going to Ireland is all about."

Did I mention that Uncle James was a wise man?

I finished my drink with him and took his advice to heart. As I was leaving, he slipped me a fiver to have another drink on the plane. You see what I mean?

I went over to Eileen's with my suitcases in tow. Michael drove me over there, and he planned to go to the airport with us. In fact, there was going to be a huge wingding in the TWA terminal. In addition to Michael, Johnny would be there with all five kids, and Eileen's aunt's family would be there with all of her grandchildren. There was a full service bar being run out of a set of coolers.

Eileen's brother Patrick and his wife Maureen were there as well, and he offered me some advice on how to deal with the ladies.

"See little and say less, Jimmy."

"Hey! My mother always says that."

"She's a wise woman, Jimmy."

I would like to report that I took Patrick's counsel to heart, but I did slip up once or twice.

The one thing that drove me crazy was leaving America at this particular time. It was a certainty that by the time I returned from Ireland, Richard Nixon would be impeached. The whole Watergate fiasco was blowing up in his face, and Tricky Dick could hear the fat lady warming up and getting ready to sing. What a time for a history major to be out of the country!

As much as I was happy that we were getting rid of Nixon, I couldn't help but wonder what would have happened if he had just come out and admitted that his campaign was a little out of control. He could have said he was sorry and then asked for the nation's forgiveness. There is no way he would have lost the election, and he wouldn't have had to resign by coming clean with the public. I guess the one good thing is that no politician will ever make that mistake again.

But now it was time to fly. Fueling had taken place, and if the plane was as fully loaded as we were, then we had no fear of running out of gas.

Eileen and I sat by ourselves. We ordered a bottle of champagne and really lived it up on our first vacation together. We saw the sunrise, and before we knew it, we were landing in Dublin. Soon I would have my first international incident in Dublin, and it involved Eileen's Aunt Catherine.

We had planned to head up to Dundalk, which is a little north of Dublin. However, the Dublin Horse Show was being held, and we just *had* to see that. I remembered the words of Patrick right about this time.

We stayed in Dublin that first day so that we could go to the horse show, and I was delighted to go to a pub and to visit the famous post office where the Irish Rebels fought the British on Easter Sunday in 1916.

Now things in Ireland were a bit tense regarding relations with the British in the North, and there was a group of IRA supporters camped out in front of the post office. I was interested in what they had to say after having had so many discussions with Uncle James over the years about his views on the subject.

When we got to talking, I noticed that they were selling memorabilia. They had this great plaque with the Irish flag and IRA logo, and it had the signatures of IRA prisoners on the back. I thought this was pretty cool, and at five pounds, it was a bargain (I think).

When I got back to my group of travelers, I was really excited about the plaque and couldn't wait to show it to everybody. Patrick's wisdom eluded me right at that moment. Aunt Catherine was beside herself and was ranting and raving. Then, as we started to leave for the fairgrounds where the horse show was being held, she yanked the plaque out of my hand and shoved it in her rather sizable handbag.

Because of the tension with the British situation, or the Troubles, as we like to say, security getting into the horse show was more than a cursory peek. They looked me over, examined my camera, and gave me a pat on the back for being a fine Yank. Aunt Catherine wasn't so lucky.

Eileen and I were already in our seats when we heard the commotion. It seemed that Aunt Catherine was having a hard time explaining to the Garda just what exactly she was doing with an IRA plaque in her handbag. Oh man, it was days before she could even look in my direction. I almost called Patrick to share this adventure. Fortunately, I was now going to be off on my own when I made my way up to Sligo.

It took me some time to get used to driving on the wrong side of the road. I know it's not the "wrong" side over there, but it sure was to me. You took your life into your hands just crossing the street. There was no way I was going to drive myself, so I checked out the train schedule and headed by rail up to my ancestral home.

The beauty of the clouds was the first thing that struck me about Ireland. They seemed to be close enough to touch. They cast such huge shadows on the mountains, and I had never experienced such beauty. Also, the fact that the daylight lasted until well past 9:00 p.m. made it that much easier to take an evening stroll to a local pub.

The only bad thing about my trip to Sligo was that Eileen was back in Dundalk with her family, but when I got back, we planned to take a long weekend trip to London.

In Sligo, I stayed in the Clarence Hotel, and I didn't know how lucky I was to get a room. It just so happened that the Yeats Festival was in full swing, and I got the absolute last room to be had. One day I will get back there to take in the festival.

I was all set to meet my Uncle Dan, the husband of my mother's sister, Aunt Katie. I had met Aunt Katie when she visited America back in 1959. I wondered if she would recognize me. Not only was I twenty-four years old, but I also had shoulder length hair. I wasn't sure how that would sit with her. I didn't have to worry.

Aunt Katie and Uncle Dan were just magnificent. They took me all around the town and introduced me as Lizzie's boy. Now Lizzie left Sligo in 1926, but the people in the town still knew who Lizzie was. I don't think anyone on Leland Avenue will know me fifty years after I leave.

I was able to see the house where my mother was born, and that was fantastic. I also had to have a wee dram of poteen. I have to say I didn't know what poteen was at the time. I soon learned that NASA developed it as an alternate fuel for the Atlas rockets that took our astronauts to the moon. It was actually Irish moonshine.

My Aunt Nora, my Uncle John's widow, made it and poured me a tiny cordial-sized glass. It burned my eyes, and I hadn't even taken a sip. Aunt Nora saw me flinch and offered a pint-sized tumbler of water to dilute it. One pint of water was not enough. Nevertheless, I drank my poteen.

We walked around the town, and one of the best parts of that was seeing Ben Bulben Mountain. This is also referred to as the Tabletop Mountain. It was so beautiful. I vowed that I would return for my thirtieth birthday.

My time in Sligo was over too soon. When Aunt Katie and Uncle Dan let me off at the train station, I had a hard time saying goodbye. In fact, I had decided I wouldn't say goodbye. I told them that I would come back to Sligo when I got back from London. I just couldn't leave them like that.

Of the many great things I experienced on my trip to Ireland, the people I met were the greatest by far. One older woman in particular did all she could to make our stay truly memorable.

Rosaline was the mother of one of Eileen's cousins, and she was our host for the time that we stayed in Dundalk. She couldn't have been nicer. From the moment I stepped into her home, I was made to feel that it was her mission in life to make me comfortable and happy.

I was "my man," and she opened her heart to me as surely as she opened her home. I couldn't help but think of Uncle James again and his advice to go out and meet the people. The others who made our trip special were another of Eileen's cousins and his wife.

Gene and Margaret Larkin lived in Crossmaglen in County Armagh located in the north of Ireland. It was here that I got a real education about the current situation in Ireland.

Eileen had made a trip to see them when I was in Sligo, so as soon as I got back, Gene and Margaret brought Eileen down to Dundalk to pick me up at the train station and to head back to Crossmaglen.

Gene and Margaret were terrific. Gene and I hit it off right away, and I couldn't help comparing him to my brother Johnny. They were both cut from the same cloth.

Gene and Margaret had a brand new house that was spectacular. It was more than a house. It was a loving home filled with three small children who could have been on the cover of an Irish travel brochure. But something just outside their house threatened the love and safety of what we enjoyed within.

There were British soldiers with automatic rifles all over the place. It was like living in a police state under martial law, and you quickly got the sense that there was no love lost between the soldiers on patrol and the citizens under their watch.

Gene took me out to the backyard to show me around. He pointed up to a hill in the distance where you could see the encampment used by the British to keep an eye on the town. Gene called it the Golan Heights. I thought that was as good a comparison as any.

The four of us stayed up all night talking; there might have been a pint or two as well, but Gene was so interesting to talk to. Listening to him tell the story of Ireland was like listening to an oral history of the Emerald Isle.

Perhaps the most poignant lesson we learned occurred after waking up the next morning. With the sounds and smells of an authentic Irish breakfast beckoning from the kitchen, the *whump*, *whump*, *whump*, of a Sikorsky helicopter served as our wake-up call. The British were not only coming, they were here and watching us from the air.

Later that day, when Margaret drove Eileen and me back to Dundalk, we were stopped and the car was searched. This would be the first time my Bronx accent served a good purpose as the soldiers, who thought I might be an IRA member on the run, only had to hear my speech to identify me as a Yank. The machine guns they were toting didn't exactly make me want to sit down and share tea and crumpets with them.

The fact that Eileen and I would be going to London the next day was starting to concern me now.

We left for Dublin the next morning and caught an Aer Lingus flight to Heathrow. Unlike our flight from America, this was more of a roller coaster ride. We went up and then quickly went down and made a smooth landing. I don't think we were in the air for more than forty-five minutes. A short cab ride later, and we were in London.

I immediately felt a connection with the people. The concern that I had felt the day before due to my encounter with British soldiers quickly dissipated. I don't know if it was because they spoke English, or rather a bizarre variety of English, or because of my love of the Beatles, or perhaps the knowledge that my grandfather was born in Manchester, but I felt a connection with the English as soon as we entered the city.

It was a strange feeling because of the bitter history of discrimination that the Irish had endured and were still enduring at the hands of my distant English cousins. Like any true American, however, I ignored the past. Not such a good thing for a would-be historian, but no one said I had to be consistent.

Eileen had a bunch of English and Irish cousins, and we had a grand time with them. After seeing the London production of *Jesus Christ Superstar*, we took a short train ride up to Teddington. There we once again met her cousin Gene who picked us up at the station and drove us to the home of his niece Bridget. She was the daughter of his brother Mickey who was also there visiting. Bridget and her husband Erwin lived in a beautiful home, and we made it there just in time for dinner.

We were all seated around a big dining room table, and Bridget immediately served pate. Eileen and I looked at each other, and it was obvious that neither of us wanted any part of pate. We loved the Liebfraumilch, however, and compelled Erwin to make several trips to his wine cellar for more. When asked if we wanted any pate, Eileen and I feigned a big dinner in town despite being famished.

When Bridget served a delicious chicken dinner a short time afterwards, she must have thought we had developed simultaneous tapeworms because we nearly ate the bones. It was a brilliant dinner, as they say in England.

After dinner, we talked and talked and talked. I looked at my watch a little nervously as the last train to London was due to leave in a few minutes. Gene, sensing my anxiety, assured me that there would be no late train in our future. Instead, he and Erwin would drive us home in Erwin's Austin Minor. Now I really relaxed, but, unfortunately, this only resulted in yet another mad dash to the wine cellar for poor Erwin.

Our London adventure came to a quick end, and we soon found ourselves in Dublin Airport heading back to Dundalk. I planned to go back to Sligo for one more trip before we headed home to New York.

Two days after returning from London, I headed to the train station in Dundalk and took a train to Dublin only to catch another train up to Sligo. Remind me never to travel so long on a train again.

Instead of staying at the Clarence Hotel, Aunt Bea, my Uncle Dan's sister, put me up for the two days that I would be in Sligo. I sure was being taken care of by the Irish ladies! She was as kind and loving as Rosaline had been, and my stay with Aunt Bea was yet another highlight of my trip.

The next day it was back to the house where my mother was born, the town where she was raised, and the church where she was baptized. Aunts, uncles, and cousins all came out to see Lizzie's boy. I went on a tour of Uncle Dan's farm and saw how they cut turf in the bog. I even got a sample of turf to bring home with me. Now all I needed was a fireplace to burn it in. But Ireland is a strange place. For a country where life is so nice and slow, and history seems to stall in its tracks, my travels seemed to move at warp speed. I soon found myself once again at the Sligo train station saying goodbye to Aunt Katie and Uncle Dan. This time it was for keeps.

The next few days would see repetitions of my farewell at the train station. They didn't get easier with practice.

I got back to Dundalk Saturday afternoon. We only had a few more days in Ireland, so Eileen and I were determined to make the most of the time we had left. While I had been to a few pubs, just a few mind you, I wanted to go to a pub on a Saturday night to have a real Irish pub experience.

We set off around 7:00 p.m. and entered a pub in Dundalk. It was what I refer to as an old man's bar. That's all who were there, old men. I had a pint, Eileen had a drink, and then we gave up and paid up. As we were about to leave the pub, the barkeep said, "You know they're having a sing upstairs." I didn't know what he meant by that, but he urged us up the stairs.

When I got to the top of the stairs, I found a door, but I really didn't hear anything. I opened the door and we were immediately accosted by the sounds and smells of a real Irish pub experience. Eileen and I looked at each other and agreed to go in.

As we made our way toward the bar, which was no easy feat, I couldn't help but notice that there were old people, people our age, and young kids all sitting together and having a grand time, just like the Rooney parties. Finally, I arrived at the bar and ordered our drinks. At the first utterance of a single syllable from my lips, there was a harmonious, cacophonous, and uproarious eruption of "HE'S A YANK!"

With that, we were summarily whisked away to a seat of honor right by the band quickly followed by two drinks for each of us. It was like we were family. They couldn't get enough of us. They even wanted me to sing!

It was a scene, man. I can't help but grin when I think about that night.

Then, just as the night was rolling and I was really feeling the Irish in me, the music stopped, the bar served no more, and when I asked what was happening, I was dumbfounded at the answer. "It's twelve o'clock, mate, the bar closes 'cause there's Mass in the morning."

There was Mass in the morning, and Gene and Margaret came down one last time to join us. We agreed to spend our last day together, and it was a grand day altogether. We talked as if we hadn't talked enough before. We drank as if—well, we had drunk enough before. Then we went out for the best dinner we had on our trip.

Gene and Margaret left us back at Rosaline's after a spectacular day. It was hard saying goodbye, but we knew we would see them again. The next day's goodbye was not so easy, either.

We arose early because we had to pack. We were getting a lift back down to Dublin Airport and would be leaving in an hour or two. Rosaline made us an outstanding Irish breakfast with plenty of brown bread and her famous strawberry rhubarb jam. I was going to miss these Irish breakfasts.

I carried the bags to the car, and then I saw the women starting to say goodbye to Rosaline. I was having a hard enough time just watching them say goodbye. I didn't know how I would manage it myself. Finally, Rosaline left the ladies and made her way over to me, saying, "Oh, my man!" That was it. I lost it, and then I hugged her and gave her a big kiss that made her smile. I knew we would never see her again.

I thought of my mother leaving home when she was only nineteen and saying goodbye to her mother, her brother, and her sister knowing she would probably never see them again. I never appreciated the hardship she had endured until that moment.

—∾—

When Eileen and I returned from Ireland, we almost immediately got back to the business of going to school. The trip to Ireland was more than a vacation as we came back to New York even more committed to each other than when we had left.

We knew that it was just a matter of time before we would be engaged and on to the serious matter of planning our life together. We had some assignments to finish first, but it was just a matter of time.

Time has always been fascinating to me. I think back to those eight years of grammar school in Blessed Sacrament as the longest eight years of my life. When I look back, even the eighth grade seems long in comparison to college and graduate school. The seasons continued to change and I got older by the second. Yet, the week still seemed to drag as I waited for Eileen to come home to me.

I wonder if Einstein had any theories to explain that.

The holidays came and went as they always do, and finally in March, while Eileen was in her last year of Saint Vincent's School of Nursing, we were engaged. The girl I had admired all night long back on that Friday in 1971 said yes to my proposal of marriage, and in a little more than a year's time, we would marry.

—∾—

September 19, 1976, the day Eileen and I would be married, began as many Sundays had in 1261 Leland Avenue, Apartment 6. Coffee was brewed, eggs were scrambled, and the Irish soda bread was buttered. My mother and father, though filled with nervous energy, avoided the conversation that hung in the air.

Like Michael, back on the eve of his wedding, Mom and Dad didn't want to acknowledge that this would be our last meal before I got married. Maybe I read too much into these events. I know that having a sense of the momentous is a good thing at important football games or when heroes say goodbye to their fans. But maybe when it comes to these kinds of life-changing, emotional points of no return, Lizzie has the best advice: Maybe we should "see little and say less."

I acquiesced to their desire to avoid the big goodbye and we talked about the Jets, the Yankees, and my upcoming trip to Bermuda with Eileen. It was a grand thing being together that morning, and the Irish soda bread never tasted better.

A few hours later, we got dressed for the wedding, me in my tux, Mom in a beautiful dress, and Dad in his favorite suit. Michael would be coming over to pick us up after dropping Margaret and their boys off at Blessed Sacrament. When Michael came into the apartment, he was one big grin. He knew exactly what I was going through, and he was enjoying every agonizing minute. I asked him if he was ready for his toast. "Oh, yeah, I've been waiting a long time for that."

Finally, we were ready to go, but I decided to let Michael take only Mom and Dad. I wanted to walk. I think they understood, and no one tried to talk me out of it. They went down the stairs, and I watched them take off in the car.

I couldn't help but look around at the place where I had spent my entire life one last time.

There was the spot I drove a hole in the wall with my baseball bat after my father had just painted the living room. There was the outlet that caught fire when I was ten, and we had to go without electricity for an entire weekend. That spot over there was where I had watched Joe Namath beat the Colts in the Super Bowl and Mickey Mantle hit the homerun off Barney Schultz in the ninth inning of the World Series.

So many memories, I couldn't possibly think of them all, and now I had to leave them all behind. But it was time to go now.

As I left my apartment at 1261 Leland Avenue, the Pelham Bay 6 train rumbled on the EL on Westchester Avenue. I turned in the opposite direction and walked toward Gleason Avenue. As I made my way to Blessed Sacrament, I surveyed all that was before me and thought I was surely in Paradise. What could be better than a beautiful day in the Bronx?

Love continued to be in the air on Leland Avenue.

CHAPTER 19

MY BACK PAGES

My life with Eileen began in 1971 and continues to this day. We were married on that sunny Sunday in 1976 at Blessed Sacrament where so much of our history took place.

Although we moved to a strange and foreign land known as Flushing, our ties to the Bronx continued to bring us home for many years afterward. In truth, we never really left the Bronx. Eventually, we merely extended its borders out to the distant shores of Eastern Long Island.

Mike and I worked together for twelve years in two different jobs, and it is due to his encouragement and loyalty that I was able to maintain a wonderful career in higher education.

While we never did find John Tent Man on Hot Dog Beach, PJ and I often do find ourselves sneaking a beer or two on the white sands of Ponquogue Beach in Hampton Bays. PJ is a successful lawyer, and he's the one who pushed me to follow him into law school. He may yet get his wish for us to renew our flat-fixing business as he still has the spoke wrench.

As for the rest of the crew, Trent and Freddie get together with us several times a year to remember what being thirteen was all about.

Mike and I continue to have season tickets to the Jets, but now we share that experience with our children and their spouses. While I don't think we considered that possibility when we first got our season tickets in the summer of 1968, we wouldn't have been surprised by it, either. We also get to a Yankees game or two.

Mike, Freddie, Trent, and I join PJ at his annual non-fishing fishing trip at his house in Hampton Bays. But we might as well still be in the schoolyard of Blessed Sacrament or hanging out on Hoch's Corner because the laughs are the same as they were fifty years ago in the wonderful land of the Bronx.

Pat and Paul have been our dearest friends since that first meeting in the vestibule of Blessed Sacrament. Whenever we needed a friend they were there.

A family that we cherish more and more as the years go by has sustained Eileen and me throughout our life together. We have weathered all of the challenges that life has a way of presenting because we had so many who supported us. Though many who are dear to us have departed, they haven't entirely left us.

Our children Sean, Jeannine, Bryan, and our daughter-in-law Maggie have continued the Newell-Rooney tradition of providing unconditional love to us. They have made a Bronx Boy and a Bronx Girl very happy and extremely proud. And while it has been written that you can't go home again, it's nice to know that our children can. Eileen and I have had the pleasure of seeing Sean, Jeannine, and Bryan return to the Bronx to attend Fordham University. It was at Fordham that Sean met Maggie so it was no surprise that when they married they chose to live in the Bronx. For her part, upon graduation Jeannine stayed in the Bronx to accept a teaching position. Bryan, too, will, no doubt one day, find his way back to the land of his ancestors. Each has his or her own stories to live and to write and it is nice to know that the Bronx will continue to inspire a new generation of tales.

Made in the USA
San Bernardino, CA
16 June 2015